Women and Water

Woven Portraits from Around the World

Jacquard Weavings by Mary E. Burns

Mary Burns

Published by: Manitowish River Press
                 4245N State Highway 47
                 Mercer, WI 54547
                 Phone: (715) 476-2828
                 E-mail: *burnsbates@gmail.com*
                 Website: *www.manitowishriverstudio.com*
                 Website: *www.manitowishriverpress.com*

Editor: Callie Bates (*www.calliebates.com*)
Book and cover design: Bev Watkins (*www.beverlyjanedesign.com*)
Photos of Weavings: Jim Schumaker (*https://natureandhumanphotography.com*)
Cover Photograph: Jim Schumaker

Publisher's Cataloging in Publication Data
Burns, Mary and Bates, John –
       Women and Water: Woven Portraits from Around the World
Artist Mary Burns, Text by John Bates
       ISBN 978-0-9998157-4-8 (softcover)
       ISBN 978-0-9998157-5-5 (eBook)
       1. Art
       2. Nature
       3. Women

Library of Congress Control Number: 2023936306

Printed in the United States.

0 9 8 7 6 5 4 3 2 1

A huge thank you to the following organizations for making this project possible:

DEDICATION

*To my mom and all the grandmothers before me, to my sisters,
to my daughters, and of course, to my incredible husband John Bates.*

To all the women working for water.

To water.

TABLE OF CONTENTS

INTRODUCTION

A Native American saying, "Water is Life," is simple, direct and true. For me, water has always been sacred. But it was through getting to know Mildred "Tinker" Schuman, an Ojibwe Elder, and many other Native women when weaving the *Ancestral Women Exhibit: Wisconsin's 12 Tribes*, that I came to understand their deep reverence for water. In many traditional cultures, women are the protectors of water, because women give birth and are seen as keepers of water.

Beginning with North American water keepers and water walkers, the idea for this exhibit spread as I found more and more people across the globe doing important water advocacy and work. They included farmers in Mozambique, scientists, oceanographers, artists, journalists, limnologists, a sea captain in the Kingdom of Tonga, a conservation biologist in the arctic, and activists in Detroit, India, Peru, and Honduras. All of these women and more are doing essential work for water, for the planet, and for us.

The exhibit features 39 woven portraits representing 38 women and 20 countries, plus the Arctic and Antarctica.

Beginning at a young age, I committed myself to the art and craft of weaving, eventually transitioning from tapestries to rug-weight pieces to handwoven Jacquard portraits. My daily practice includes centering myself in the natural and spiritual world, designing, weaving, and creating with yarns and threads. It is this lifetime of work that has enabled me to create this exhibit inspired by these extraordinary women. Beginning in 2016, I started researching and connecting with women and organizations. In 2017 I threw the first shuttle of the first portrait for this exhibit. Today, April 22, 2023, I completed the 29th. In that time, I have thrown shuttles approximately 70,000 times and spent countless hours designing. I wove these 31" x 42" portraits by hand on my TC-2 Jacquard loom, Brigid, with cotton threads.

In many cultures, fiber arts are seen as a traditionally feminine craft. Creating these portraits through a woven medium reflects the often-underestimated power and importance of women's work.

I am blessed and humbled to do this work and am so grateful to the people of *Women and Water: Woven Portraits from Around the World.* They are role models of strength, fortitude, sacrifice and love. It is my great honor to present them to you. I only wish I could have woven more—there are so many women who should also be honored for their water work.

May these women and their stories encourage you to strengthen your own ties with water and inspire you to take action to protect our waters.

Mary Burns
April 22, 2023

~~~

"Warrior up for water for all!"
Monica Lewis-Patrick, Water Warrior of Detroit

"No blue, no green."
Sylvia Earle

Women and Water
Woven Portraits from Around the World

ALASKA
- Victoria Qutuuq Buschman *(Arctic)*

ONTARIO, CANADA
- Grandmother Josephine Mandamin-Ba
- Autumn Peltier

UNITED STATES
- Sylvia Earle, *California*
- Sandra Postel, *Washington*
- Mary Alice McWhinnie, *Illinois (Antarctica)*
- Tinker Schuman, *Wisconsin*
- Monica Lewis-Patrick, *Michigan*
- Gretchen Gerrish, *Wisconsin*
- Rachel Carson, *Maryland*
- Carol Warden and Emily Stanley, *Wisconsin*
- Sharon Day, *Minnesota*
- Wilma Mankiller, *Oklahoma*
- Marjory Stoneman Douglas, *Florida*

HONDURAS
- Berta Cáceres

PERU
- Ruth Buendía

IRELAND
- Brigid, Goddess and Saint

WALES
- Kathleen Carpenter

SIBERIA, RUSSIA

INDIA

SRI LANKA

INDONESIA

KENYA

ACARE/A WIS, AFRICAN GREAT LAKES

MOZAMBIQUE

KINGDOM OF TONGA

NEW ZEALAND

SIBERIA, RUSSIA
• Marina Rikhvanova

INDIA
• Nafisa Barot

SRI LANKA
• Asha de Vos

INDONESIA
• Aleta Baun

KENYA
• Ikal Angelei

ACARE/A WIS, AFRICAN GREAT LAKES
• Catherine Ajuna Fridolin
• Elizabeth Wambui Wanderi
• Margret Sindat
• Donnata Alupot
• Marie Claire Dusabe
• Diane Umutoni
• Grite Nelson Mwaijengo
• Gladys Chigamba
• Ester Kagoya

MOZAMBIQUE
• Vaida Furanguene
• Fatianca Paulino
• Querida Baringuinha

KINGDOM OF TONGA
• Aunofo Havea Funaki

NEW ZEALAND
• Tāwera Tahuri

NAFISA BAROT

Nafisa Barot ~ India

Photo courtesy of Utthan Gujarat

Some moments in life change everything. During a visit to the village of Jhankhi in western India, Nafisa Barot writes, "I will never forget what I saw. There was a child of about four who was extremely dehydrated and looked like she was going to die soon. I asked her mother for some water to be brought. She left and returned half an hour later with half a glass of muddy water. I knew there was a water problem in the area but I asked her to get more water. She got only a little more. I got angry and asked her what kind of a mother she was for behaving like this. She immediately broke down. A lady beside her told me that the mother had given the water which she had kept for the following day. I just started crying and gave her whatever water I had. This is something that has always remained with me. After a couple of days the child died."

"When water finally came, hundreds of women rushed to the tank to fill their vessels. They all had to fight to get two or three pots filled in an unbelievable conflict, resulting in blood dropping into the water."

And then there was this: "The temperature in the Bhal region of Dhandhuka near the coast of western India must have been about 48°C (118°F), when Devuben from Mingalpur walked from her home to a remote water tank, carrying empty pots. The saline-parched land must have burnt her bare feet. She stood at the empty groundwater tank and prayed for some water through the broken pipe. The government had installed a 100 km-long pipeline to bring water to this tank. It had been three days since any water had come through the pipeline, and the anxiety, anger and frustration could be seen on her face.

"When water finally came, hundreds of women rushed to the tank to fill their vessels. They all had to fight to get two or three pots filled in an unbelievable conflict, resulting in blood dropping into the water. Devuben only managed to get whatever was left at the bottom of the tank. Being a Dalit, the lowest caste in India, she could not even jostle like others. She had to content herself with one-and-a-half pots of muddy water."

Unfortunately, this wasn't anything new: "For women water was the major preoccupation for their entire day. It seemed their whole life was centered around getting enough water for the family and their cattle."

With these moments burned in her mind, in 1981, Barot co-founded *Utthan* ("upliftment" in Hindi) with three other women, an organization to help address women's, and all people's, rights to regular, safe drinking water. In doing so, they had to also challenge a deep patriarchy, feudal exploitation, and caste discrimination at local and national levels.

One of Utthan's first major interventions was raising their voice against centralized piped water, and instead promoting local water resources. Villages in the area were getting water sourced from over 60 miles away through a World Bank funded pipeline. Unfortunately, villages at the tail end of the pipeline got water only intermittently every couple of days, which often led to violent confrontations. Traditional ponds in the area had also run dry as a result of the digging of borewells by better-off farmers for cash crops.

In 1985, Utthan, along with another organization, Mahiti, proposed harvesting rainwater in lined ponds in the saline area of Bhal, which resulted in a great success. "What we did was to take up 20 hectares of 'waste land' from the government on which to experiment," Barot explained. "Using traditional knowledge from the area, we experimented by digging a pond and lining the bottom and sides of it with low density polyethylene. This was covered with a layer of 'sweet' (salt free) soil on the bottom and brick and lime on the sides."

The polyethylene prevented saline groundwater from mixing with rainwater runoff.

Seeing this success, other communities then demanded the government invest money in this alternative, which was met with resistance from both the government and by the men in the villages who believed they knew better.

In the face of all this resistance, women raised their voices, demanding acceptance and implementation of their alternative plans. They challenged the moneylenders and feudal lords who were running water tankers to haul water and who had a great stake in continuing the tanker-supplied water system that created a great dependency on them.

The women leaders also had to confront the deeply entrenched caste system. For them, the struggle for access to reliable water systems became the means to bring all women together on one platform against discrimination and inequality.

Finally, in 1987, the government gave funds for constructing eight lined ponds in eight villages of Bhal.

However, the women's struggle was far from over. The women refused to have the ponds located by the government engineers or by their male community leaders who wanted to have the ponds near their farms, so that they could use the water for agriculture. Women's groups wanted sites that were closer to their homes, so that they could have easier access to safe water and keep an eye on the ponds.

They won.

Since then, women have advocated for trying out new ideas, such as sub-surface check dams and solar distillation rooftop water tanks. For example, women from Dahod and Panchmahal districts of Gujarat have been ardent promoters of groundwater recharging and decentralized water systems in the hilly regions and have mobilized communities to share their private wells for the sake of drinking water for all.

The struggle for clean water was nearly universal and continued in impoverished communities, whatever their cultural leanings. However, an outbreak of violence against Muslim communities in Gujurat in 2002 resulted in the deaths of an estimated 3,500 people, creating enormous divides between the Hindu and Muslim communities. Now Muslim women standing in line for water were pushed back and bypassed. Men had to accompany Muslim women to protect them from sexual violence when they went to outdoor bathrooms. And within Muslim families, patriarchy grew to a level where women became confined to indoors.

Utthan started organizing women leaders from these diverse communities around water issues as a means of bridging the divides by addressing common needs. A women's group emerged from the mixed communities, and together they built 10 sources of drinking water, some 250 toilets, and three bathing places.

Utthan has directly touched the lives of more than 1.4 million people of 412 villages in six districts of Gujarat. They've facilitated providing over 360,000 people with sustainable and equitable access to safe water and facilitated the adoption of eco-sanitation toilets with more than 300 families and 225 toilets catering to people with disabilities.

All this work led Barot to win the 2020 International Water Association's Women in Water Award.

Barot writes, "Why are women so passionately engaged in the struggle for accessing water? Is it due to their 'intrinsic role' as water providers in the family resulting from patriarchal social systems or is it because women see water as a means to fight injustice and inequality and have a better understanding of the issue, socially and politically? It is certainly both . . . Unless you build communities from within, nothing is going to change."

(Note: As of 2020, two billion people still lacked daily access to a reliable source of drinking water. By 2050, the estimated number of people who will struggle to get water for at least one month every year will swell to five billion.)

"Unless you build communities from within, nothing is going to change."

Photos courtesy of Utthan Gujarat

BERTA CÁCERES

Berta Cáceres ~ Honduras

Photo courtesy of Goldman Environmental Prize

In 2015, Berta Cáceres won the world's foremost prize for environmental defenders, the Goldman Environmental Prize, for rallying the indigenous Lenca people of Honduras to successfully stop the construction of a dam from flooding their lands. Foretelling her own fate, Cáceres dedicated the award to the dozens of "martyrs" who had earlier given their lives to protect Honduras' rivers, lands and mineral resources. Between 2010 and 2014, 101 environmental activists were killed in Honduras, making it the most dangerous country in the world, relative to its size, for environmental activists.

"Energy is not just a technical issue, it's a political issue to do with life, territories, sovereignty and the right to community self-determination. We believe this is the moment to profoundly debate capitalism and how energy is part of the domination of indigenous communities and violation of their rights ...That's what Lenca communities like Río Blanco are living through right now."

Less than a year after receiving the Goldman award, Cáceres was murdered in her bedroom by two hired gunmen.

Twelve days after her assassination her colleague Nelson García was also killed. Then another activist was murdered before the month was out.

To understand how all this came to be, we need to step back. Cáceres had co-founded the Council of Popular and Indigenous Organizations of Honduras (COPINH), an organization to support indigenous people's rights in Honduras in 1993, and was active in it for more than a decade. She learned in 2006 that the developers of the dam, a joint project of Honduran company Desarrollos Energéticos SA (DESA) and Chinese state-owned Sinohydro, the world's largest dam developer, had breached international law by failing to consult with the local people whose traditional way of life would be destroyed by the dam.

Cáceres, known as "The Guardian of the Rivers," organized fierce protests of DESA and the hydroelectric dam that the company was building. The campaign also reached out to the international community, bringing the case to the Inter-American Human Rights Commission and lodging appeals against the project's funders such as the International Finance Corporation (IFC), the private sector arm of the World Bank.

To make matters worse for the Honduran people, in 2009, a U.S. backed military coup overthrew the democratically-elected government, installed a new government, and Honduras witnessed an explosive growth in environmentally destructive megaprojects that would displace indigenous communities.

In 2010, the Honduran Congress passed a law that awarded contracts to a group of private companies, including DESA and Sinohydro, to build hundreds of additional hydroelectric dams throughout the country. Almost 30 percent of the country's land had been earmarked for mining concessions, creating a demand for cheap energy to power the mining operations. Four of the approved dams were known collectively as the Agua Zarca Dams, and were to be built along the Gualcarque

River, in western Honduras, on territory inhabited by the indigenous Lenca people.

After DESA continued to build the dams despite the many protests, supporters of COPINH and members of the local communities blocked the roads to one of the dams in April of 2013, withstanding multiple eviction attempts and violent attacks from militarized security contractors and the Honduran armed forces. Tomas Garcia, a community leader from Rio Blanco, was shot and killed during a peaceful protest, while others were attacked, discredited, detained, and even tortured.

Cáceres's response: "They are afraid of us because we are not afraid of them."

DESA also launched trumped-up criminal cases against her, first for possession of an unlicensed gun and later for incitement. Death threats against Cáceres, a mother of four, and COPINH were constant, all coming from people working for, or with, DESA. Dozens of regional and international organizations called upon the Honduran government to stop criminalizing the defense of human rights and to investigate threats against the protestors.

The government did nothing to stop the violence. The thugs who beat up, intimidated, and even evicted Lenca residents were given cover by federal troops, who often broke up peaceable demonstrations themselves.

In an interview, Cáceres said, "The army has an assassination list of 18 wanted human rights fighters with my name at the top. I want to live. There are many things I still want to do in this world but I have never once considered giving up fighting for our territory, for a life with dignity, because our fight is legitimate. I take lots of care, but in the end, in this country where there is total impunity, I am vulnerable…When they want to kill me, they will do it."

In 2013, Cáceres sent her children abroad to study on scholarships in Argentina and Mexico, so they couldn't be used as pawns by her enemies.

Cáceres and the Lenca community persevered, their efforts successfully keeping construction equipment out of the proposed dam site. And in late 2013, Sinohydro terminated its contract with DESA, publicly citing ongoing community resistance and outrage following Tomas Garcia's death. Soon after, the IFC withdrew its funding, also citing concerns about human rights violations.

The death threats escalated. After Cáceres's murder in 2016, international outrage sparked Dutch development bank FMO and FinnFund to suspend their involvement in the Agua Zarca project.

In June 2016, a former soldier with the US-trained special forces units of the Honduran military confirmed that Cáceres's name was on their hitlist months before her assassination.

Gustavo Cáceres, Berta's brother, partnered with organizations like the Association for a More Just Society and Oxfam to make sure the Attorney General's investigation into Cáceres's murder moved forward. They coordinated a trip to Washington, D.C. where they met with Congressional representatives, including Speaker of the House Nancy Pelosi.

Their efforts paid off. In 2018, a Honduran court ruled that executives of DESA ordered the killing of Cáceres.

In 2019, seven men were found guilty of the murder and sentenced to 30 to 50 years. Three of the eight arrested people were linked to US-trained elite military troops.

In 2021, David Castillo, former president of DESA, was found guilty in an unanimous ruling by the Honduran Supreme Court of plotting the assassination of Berta Cáceres. Castillo used paid informants and military contacts to monitor Cáceres, and then coordinated and paid for the assassination. While this was a remarkable conviction in a country not known for fair trials, evidence came out during the trial that points to the involvement of yet others much more powerful.

In 2021, the "Berta Cáceres Human Rights in Honduras Act" was introduced into the U.S. House of Representatives. This bill prohibits U.S. assistance to the police or military of Honduras, and states that the Department of the Treasury shall instruct U.S. representatives of multilateral development banks to vote against providing loans to the Honduran police or military. The prohibition shall only be lifted if the Department of State certifies to Congress that various conditions have been met, including that the Honduran government has (1) pursued all legal avenues to reach verdicts in specified crimes, such as the killings of indigenous land-rights activist Berta Cáceres and of 100 small-farmer activists in the Aguan Valley; (2) investigated and prosecuted members of the military and police who have violated human rights; and (3) taken effective steps to establish the rule of law.

The bill still awaits a vote.

In this portrait, Berta Cáceres is flanked by her mother, Austra Bertha Flores Lopez, who is a midwife, social activist, and role model of humanitarianism. Violence swept through neighboring El Salvador in the 1980s, and Austra Flores took in and cared for the refugees fleeing the violence. She provided medical care for thousands of underserved indigenous people who had nowhere else to turn for care. She was later elected and served as a two-term mayor of their hometown of La Esperanza, then as a congresswoman, and finally as a governor of the state of Intibucá.

She continues to this day to fight for indigenous rights.

And as of 2023, the dam project remains frozen.

SACRED GUALCARQUE RIVER

Photo courtesy of Goldman Environmental Prize

"I want to live. There are many things I still want to do in this world but I have never once considered giving up fighting for our territory, for a life with dignity, because our fight is legitimate. I take lots of care but in the end, in this country where there is total impunity, I am vulnerable...When they want to kill me, they will do it."

SYLVIA EARLE

Sylvia Earle ~ California, USA

"No blue, no green."

It's that simple, says Dr. Sylvia Earle, Explorer-in-Residence for the National Geographic Society and one of the world's most recognized proponents for ocean conservation. "We need to do everything in our power to protect and restore what we can [of the ocean] as if our lives depend on it, because they do...The single non-negotiable thing life requires is water."

To summarize Earle's life via her extraordinary list of awards, prizes, recognitions, book titles and honorary degrees is daunting. Among other things, she's been dubbed "Her Deepness" by the *New York Times*, a "Living Legend" by the Library of Congress, and the first "Hero for the Planet" by *Time Magazine*.

"We need to do everything in our power to protect and restore what we can [of the ocean] as if our lives depend on it, because they do...The single non-negotiable thing life requires is water."

But perhaps most telling of her passion for ocean life, at least in her younger years, was her work for her PhD dissertation from Duke University where she collected more than 20,000 samples of algae from the Gulf of Mexico to catalog aquatic plant life. She writes, "The dominant diversity of life on earth, contrary to what some people think, is not rainforests, as wonderfully diverse as they are. It's the ocean!"

Still, other highlights of her life must be noted, including holding the world record for the deepest untethered dive, creating her own line of deep-sea submersibles, and working as the former chief scientist for the National Oceanic and Atmospheric Administration. She is also the founder of SEAlliance, which partnered with *National Geographic* on Mission Blue to further global initiatives aimed at restoring health and productivity to the ocean.

Earle launched Mission Blue in 2009 to establish marine protected areas (dubbed Hope Spots) around the globe in order to achieve 30% protection of the ocean by

Hope Spots, Map by Mission Blue

2030. (See the Emmy Award-winning Netflix documentary, *Mission Blue.*) More than two hundred organizations have supported this mission, and Mission Blue has created 150 Hope Spots to date (2023) covering over 57 million square kilometers around the world. These myriad Hope Spots safeguard biodiversity and offer the basic life support services that provide resiliency to counter confounding issues like over-harvesting fish, plastics, various sources of pollution, and accelerating climate change.

What's the idea behind Hope Spots when it comes to seafood? "That you can have your fish and eat them, too, if you have large protected areas in the oceans that give them a chance, where you simply don't take the fish. The ocean has given us so much for so long; it's time for us to return the favor."

Earle has led more than 100 expeditions, logged over 7,000 hours underwater, lectured in over 70 countries and authored more than 200 scientific, technical, and popular publications. Now 87 years old (she was born in 1935) and still diving, she's learned that "Protecting nature is no longer viewed as an option but as a necessity. We have no other choice. We must maintain the integrity of the natural systems that hold our planet steady."

Earle speaks of our oceans with wonder and amazement, and calls them "the blue heart of the planet." Sadly, she's witnessed enormous changes over her career. "In my short lifetime, I have seen the degradation of nature on an unprecedented scale. In the 50 years since I took my first dive in the Keys, the world has lost half of its coral reefs...By the end of the 20th century, up to 90 percent of the sharks, tuna, swordfish, marlins, groupers, turtles, whales, and many other large creatures that prospered in the Gulf of Mexico for millions of years had been depleted by overfishing...Ocean acidification as a consequence of excess carbon dioxide that is entering the sea...is bad news, for everything, including the basic life support functions that we take for granted...We are seeing an ever-increasing avalanche of plastics in the ocean. We are seeing a heap of indifference."

She notes that the number one problem that underlies all these issues is communication, the "lack of people, generally speaking, knowing why the ocean matters, knowing what we're doing to the ocean, seeing the cause and effect relationship between the decline of the ocean and the perils that presents to the future of human civilization." She says plainly, "Until we make that connection, until people know why they should care, and then affirmatively take action as a result of knowing, we're going to see a continued move in the direction of decline."

There's good news among the bad. "I'm no longer hearing people say, 'Woe is me; look at what we've lost.' People are waking up and seeing a tremendous opportunity, not just to save what's left, but to reverse the decline and help nature heal."

"There is a growing awareness, which is the best way to counter indifference. People who know might care. They can't care if they don't know. They might not care even if they do know, but they can't if they don't know what the issues are. So I'll say it again: The next 10 years will be the most important in the next 10,000 years in terms of shaping a future where humans can have a hope for an enduring place within the natural systems that keep us alive."

She's often asked how much needs to be protected. "So far, the part of the planet that is fully protected...is just barely creeping up on one percent...that is, where even the fish are safe...So suppose you said, 'I'm only going to protect one percent of my heart.' Is that enough? How much is enough? Well, I think we need to respect all of it. And, like the doctor who is treating a sick patient, first do no harm with your actions. Do everything you can to take care of the vital systems that keep us alive. That means looking at the ocean with new eyes, looking at the fish with new eyes, looking at what we're putting in the ocean, with respect to dumping, whether it is garbage or sewage or whatever. Treat it as if your life depends on it, because your life really *does* depend on it.

"The finest and best use of the ocean is not what we can take from it to eat. It's our existence that we take from the ocean that is the highest and most important thing.

"We are at that point in history where, as never before, we've got knowledge available that did not exist even five years ago, and the ability to communicate in ways that didn't exist until quite recently. So I consider this a sweet spot in time. We're right at this crossroads, and I'm not alone in observing the urgency of taking the knowledge we have and applying it to ensure that we can do the best we can with it."

To reiterate: "No blue, no green... Take care of the ocean as if your life depends on it, because it does."

"The finest and best use of the ocean is not what we can take from it to eat. It's our existence that we take from the ocean that is the highest and most important thing."

Photo by US Fish and Wildlife Service

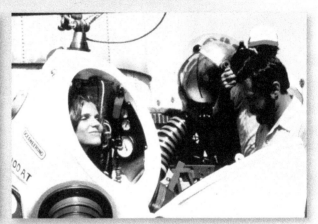

Photo by OAR/National Undersea Research Program (NURP)

Official White House Photo by Pete Souza

U.S. President Barack Obama talks to oceanographer Dr. Sylvia Earle, National Geographic Society Explorer-in-Residence, during a visit to Midway Atoll, September 1, 2016 in the Papahanaumokuakea Marine National Monument, Northwestern Hawaiian Islands.

ASHA DE VOS

Asha de Vos ~ Sri Lanka

Photo courtesy of Asha de Vos

Asha de Vos, Sri Lanka's first and only marine biologist, found it anything but easy to become one. Gender equality in Sri Lanka was, and still is, a rarity. "My mother took me aside when I was about six years old and said, You know what? If we can afford to educate only one child, it will be you. Because your brother is a boy, the system will help him to help himself and he will find his way. Therefore, you need to stand on your own feet.

"My life kick-started when I knew my value. I knew that my family didn't see me as different just because I was not a boy—that is what I grew up with. As for me, nothing was impossible."

"We work to shift the current marine conservation trajectory by inspiring and creating opportunities for the next generation of diverse ocean heroes —those individuals who were overlooked or not considered an important part of the team in the past...If we truly want to save our oceans, never forget: every coastline needs a local hero."

She would look through the pages of second-hand *National Geographic* magazines and "imagine that that would be me one day—going places where no-one else would ever go and seeing things no-one else would ever see," inspiring her to dream of being an "adventure-scientist."

She went on to receive degrees from the University of St. Andrews, the University of Oxford, and the University of Western Australia, and founded the Sri Lankan Blue Whale Project in 2008, the first long-term study on blue whales within the northern Indian Ocean. She had discovered that a unique population of blue whales, previously thought to migrate every year, stayed in waters near Sri Lanka year-round, a remarkable discovery because this is the only non-migratory population of blue whales in the world. Due to her research, the International Whaling Commission designated Sri Lankan blue whales as a species in urgent need of conservation, and it now collaborates with the Sri Lankan government on preventing whale ship-strikes.

The project ultimately blossomed into Oceanswell, a much larger marine science organization that de Vos leads, blending research, education, and conservation advocacy focused on Sri Lanka and its surrounding waters.

Sri Lanka is an island nation with more than 8,000 square miles of territorial waters, home to 29 documented species of marine mammals, including five large whale species. But until de Vos came along, very little was known in Sri Lanka about these creatures or, for that matter, about marine biology. She notes, "Seventy percent of our [global] coastlines are in the developing world, but representation at the global stage is disproportional. Despite coming from a tropical island with jurisdiction over eight times more ocean area than land area, most people had never heard of, let alone met, a marine biologist. Historically, countries like mine used the ocean as a space of extraction and not protection. Studying to become a marine biologist was not, and still is not, possible in my island home."

Then there was the island's patriarchy to contend with. "Even when I tell people I am a marine biologist, so many people turn around and say, 'Isn't that a man's job?' In reply I also say, You know what? Before I started doing that job in this country, it was no one's job— not a man or a woman."

She also faced an uphill battle as a woman from the global south in a field that remains dominated by those from developed countries. "The challenge is that marine conservation is very, very Western-centric: almost perceived as a field that belongs in the developed world. So I had to prove myself, not just as a woman, but as a locally grown woman...

"When I first discovered this population of whales and suspected that they did not undertake long-range migrations to cold places to feed, the only experienced people [in whale research] lived across the globe from me," she says. "As I described what I had seen, many of them wanted to come do the research themselves. It felt like they did not believe people from my part of the world had the capacity to do what needed to be done."

De Vos contends that the practice of "parachute science," in which Western researchers drop into developing countries to collect data and leave without training or investing in the region, not only harms communities, it cripples conservation efforts. "Local people, they live on those coastlines. They speak the languages, and they see the problems every day. They [also] may be part of the problem.

"There is a community aspect to it...If we want to protect what is on all of these coastlines, we can't have parachute science happening. We can't have people from outside coming into our countries, doing work and leaving, because there is no sustainability in that model."

De Vos's capabilities have been amply recognized. Her life has included many firsts, including being the first and only Sri Lankan to have a PhD in Marine Mammal research. She's also the first Pew Fellow in Marine Conservation from Sri Lanka, as well as the first National Geographic Explorer from Sri Lanka.

She's a TED Senior Fellow as well, an Ocean Conservation Fellow at the New England Aquarium, a Duke Global Fellow in Marine Conservation, and a World Economic Forum Young Global Leader.

In 2018, she won the WingsWorldQuest Woman of Discovery at Sea award which recognizes extraordinary women making significant contributions to world knowledge and science through exploration. That same year, de Vos was named one of Asia's sustainability superwomen, listed on the BBC 100 Women 2018 list of most inspiring and influential women from around the world, and named *Lanka Monthly Digest's* Sri Lankan of the Year.

In 2020, *Scuba Diving* magazine named her a Sea Hero. And in 2021, de Vos was awarded a Vanithaabimani lifetime achievement award for outstanding accomplishments in her field and for bringing pride to her island nation.

Her life's work is now to change the current marine conservation model, protect this unique population of blue whales, and inspire the next generation of ocean heroes from all corners of the globe.

When asked what advice she would give young women today, she says, "Try to be defined not by your gender but by your capacity. The harder you work, and the more you throw yourself into something you're passionate about, the more your work starts to speak for itself...Today, nobody cares what I am. I'm a necessity: The system needs me to help to make changes. I would say to any girl out there, that's what you want to aim for—to be defined not by your gender but by your capabilities."

Photos courtesy of Asha de Vos

"The challenge is that marine conservation is very, very Western-centric: almost perceived as a field that belongs in the developed world. So I had to prove myself, not just as a woman, but as a locally grown woman..."

GRANDMOTHER JOSEPHINE MANDAMIN-BA

Grandmother Josephine Mandamin-Ba
~ Ontario, Canada

In 2000, during a Sundance Ceremony at Pipestone, Minnesota, Grand Chief E. Benton-Banaise-Bawdwayadun, an Anishinaabe elder, warned that "the day will come when an ounce of water will cost as much as gold." He looked around and asked the audience, "What are you going to do about it?"

Grandmother (*Nakomis*) Josephine Mandamin-Ba, also known as *Biidaasige-ba* ("the one who comes with the light"), was there that day and took it to heart. In Anishinaabekwe culture, women are given the responsibility to take care of the water. She soon had a dream which inspired her to call her closest friends to discuss their responsibility to pray for and protect *Nibi*, the water. From that sharing, they formed the Mother Earth Water Walkers. In this work, they envisioned women leading ceremonial journeys, carrying a copper vessel filled with water from one place to the next. The water would continually move throughout the course of the day, like walking with a water stream, with men supporting the women by carrying an eagle staff beside them and acting as their caretakers and protectors.

"The water of Mother Earth carries life to us, and as women we carry life through our bodies. We as women are life-givers, protectors of the water, and that's why we are very inclined to give Mother Earth the respect that she needs for the water."

Thus began the first of 13 Water Walks that Grandmother Josephine-Ba led during her life, walks that would take her to the Atlantic and Pacific Oceans, around the Great Lakes, and along many major rivers like the St. Lawrence.

During her first Water Walk in 2003, Mandamin-Ba wrote: "We did it for the water, for the earth, for the animals, for the insects, for the trees, for all the two-leggeds...They will know, as Mother Earth knows, that we walked with the water for all of creation."

In later writings and talks, Mandamin-Ba shared that "Water has to live, it can hear, it can sense what we're saying, it can really, really, speak to us. Some songs come to us through the water. We have to understand that water is very precious...That's our responsibility, our role, and our duty, to pass on the knowledge and understanding of water, to all people, not just Anishinabe people, but people of all colors."

Along with groups of Anishinabe and other supporters, Grandmother Josephine-Ba walked around Lake Superior in 2003, Lake Michigan in 2004, Lake Huron in 2005, Lake Ontario in 2006, Lake Erie in 2007, and Lake Michigan in 2008.

At the age of 75, Mandamin-Ba organized her final water walk, which took place in 2017 beginning in Duluth, MN, and traveled along the St. Lawrence Seaway to Matane, Quebec Canada where the Saint Lawrence River connects to the Labrador Sea and the North Atlantic Ocean. The journey lasted 97 days and covered 3,197 miles, with over 6,394,000 footsteps taken for the water.

Born in Wikwemikong Unceded Territory on Manitoulin Island in Ontario, Grandmother Josephine-Ba resided in Thunder Bay, Ontario. It's estimated she walked 15,000 miles, or nearly halfway around the circumference of the Earth. She went through three knees and 11 pairs of sneakers walking for Nibi.

Mandamin-Ba knew that "The water of Mother Earth carries life to us, and as women we carry life through our bodies. We as women are life-givers, protectors of the water, and that's why we are very inclined to give Mother Earth the respect that she needs for the water."

By the time Grandmother Josephine-Ba died in 2019 at the age of 77, she was deeply respected as a world-renowned water-rights activist. Her work is carried on by many others including Autumn Peltier, her grandniece, and through a group called *Nibi Emosaawdamajig* (Those Who Walk for the Water), led by Shirley Williams and her niece Elizabeth Osawamick.

"We did it for the water, for the earth, for the animals, for the insects, for the trees, for all the two-leggeds... They will know, as Mother Earth knows, that we walked with the water for all of creation."

Grandmother Josephine-Ba and Mary: Photo courtesy of Mary Burns

SANDRA POSTEL

Sandra Postel ~ Washington, USA

Sandra Postel offers two things seldom found in environmental literature these days: Hope and proven ways to change hope into reality. She wants everyone to know that "We have the capacity to write a new water story."

A new story—what does that mean?

In part, it means this: "We have barely tapped the innovative ways we can do more with less water—and then give some water back to nature...A future of depleted rivers, dried-up wetlands, and toxic dead zones is not inevitable. Yes, the water cycle is broken, but one river, one wetland, one city, one farm at a time, we can begin to fix it."

"We talk about water as a 'right,' but it is really the planet's greatest gift. A gift to be shared with all of life. I believe we have an ethical responsibility to manage water in such a way that all living beings, human and non-human, receive the water they need to survive...That may sound radical, but it's not. It recognizes our interdependence with the rest of life on the planet."

And then this: "Working with, rather than against, nature, pioneering cities, farmers, businesses, and conservationists are rejuvenating watersheds and floodplains, and replenishing rivers, groundwater, and soils. The result is a smarter way to mitigate flood damages, prepare for droughts, restore habitats, grow food, augment water supplies, and generally strengthen water security...Investing in a healthier water cycle, it turns out, may be the best insurance policy money can buy in this century of rapid change."

Her distinguished vitae stretches over 40 years and offers considerable credibility to her vision. Most recently in 2021, Postel received the prestigious Stockholm Water Prize, often described as the Nobel Prize for water. The nominating committee said about her: "No one has exhibited more commitment, capacity, courage, and perseverance to address far-ranging and critical water issues that affect both human and natural ecosystems."

Postel first became widely known in policy and conservation circles in 1992 when she published the book *Last Oasis: Facing Water Scarcity*. The book, printed in eight languages and made into a television documentary, was one of the first to warn about our global water crisis and to call for conservation of water-based ecosystems. She later authored two other widely respected books, *Pillar of Sand: Can the Irrigation Miracle Last?*, and *Replenish: The Virtuous Cycle of Water and Prosperity*. She is also co-author with Brian Richter of *Rivers for Life: Managing Water for People and Nature*, and the co-author with Lester Brown and Christopher Flavin of *Saving the Planet: How to Shape an Environmentally Sustainable Global Economy*. She has additionally written numerous articles for popular and scholarly publications, including *Science, Natural History, Foreign Policy*, and *The New York Times*. Her article "Troubled Waters" was selected for the 2001 edition of *Best American Science* and *Nature Writing*.

From 2009-2015, Postel served as Freshwater Fellow of the National Geographic Society, where she co-created "Change the Course." This water stewardship initiative was awarded the 2017 U.S. Water Prize for restoring billions of gallons of water to depleted rivers, aquifers and wetlands. Change the Course brings together the public, the business community, and on-the-ground conservation organizations to do the two things necessary to build water security: shrink our human water footprint and restore water to the natural world. As of 2022, 130 water stewardship projects have been supported across 22 U.S. states, Mexico, and Canada.

Through the Global Water Policy Project, which she founded in 1994, Postel has worked to bridge water science, policy and practice. She refuses to accept the old dichotomy that pits the environment versus jobs. "By getting smarter about how we use water, we can have healthy rivers, productive agriculture, and vibrant economies side by side. What gives me hope is that we can point to farmers, ranchers, cities, and businesses that are making a difference and showing that we can live more harmoniously with nature and its freshwater ecosystems. The challenge is to learn from these experiences, adapt them to new situations, and scale up these solutions...A new mind-set about water is taking shape. It's one that blends engineering, ecology, economics, and related fields into a more holistic approach that recognizes the fundamental value of nature's services."

She continues, "For a couple centuries we've been trading nature's services for engineering works—for example, building levees to control floods rather than letting natural floodplains do that work...If we refer to rivers and lakes as 'water resources,' we immediately think of them in a utilitarian way—that they're there for us to use and take as we see fit, much the way we think of oil or coal. It's important that we think of a river as a living, flowing part of nature that sustains life. Yes, a river can be a 'resource' for the generation of energy and the provision of water supplies, but most fundamentally, it's a river."

She is, however, a clear-eyed realist regarding the situation we're in: "The combination of dams, diversions, pollution, and climate change puts more and more species in peril...The population of freshwater vertebrates —such as fish and frogs—are down 83 percent compared to 50 years ago. Try to get your head around that; for every hundred fish and frogs that were around in 1970, there are now only 17. We are only starting to understand how we have impacted ecosystems and what the consequences will be...We live on a finite planet with finite water. As the basis of life, water needs to be shared with all of life."

In addition, she points out, "we will experience climate change largely through the water cycle—more intense floods and droughts, wildfires that threaten drinking water sources, glacial melting, and more toxic algal blooms in lakes and bays. With climate change, we are outside historic norms and can no longer have confidence that the dams and levees are going to hold or that the reservoirs are going to fill again. We have three existential crises happening at the same time—water shortages, biodiversity loss, and climate change. And they are interconnected, so the good news is that by working more with nature—for example, preparing for bigger floods by strategically reconnecting rivers with their natural floodplains rather than raising levees even higher—we can mitigate these three existential crises at the same time. And this is critically important because we don't have time to solve them in a piece-meal fashion."

Finally, Postel says it comes down to ethics and, ultimately, empathy. "We talk about water as a 'right,' but it is really the planet's greatest gift. A gift to be shared with all of life. I believe we have an ethical responsibility to manage water in such a way that all living beings, human and non-human, receive the water they need to survive...That may sound radical, but it's not. It recognizes our interdependence with the rest of life on the planet."

"We talk about water as a 'right,' but it is really the planet's greatest gift. A gift to be shared with all of life."

Photo by Tamara Gadzia, courtesy of Sandra Postel

Photo by Cheryl Zook/National Geographic, courtesy of Sandra Postel

VAIDA FURANGUENE
FATIANCA PAULINO
QUERIDA BARINGUINHA

*Vaida Furanguene, Fatianca Paulino
and Querida Baringuinha
~ Gorongosa National Park, Mozambique*

During a civil war in Mozambique, Vaida Furanguene, Fatianca Paulino, and Querida Baringuinha, carried water up a mountainside in Gorongosa National Park every night for a year to water newly planted coffee plants.

To understand how important their story is, we have to step back.

Gorongosa National Park was touted in the 1970s as one of Africa's most spectacular national parks, with massive herds of wildlife roaming its Rift Valley grasslands and woodlands. Famed biologist Edward O. Wilson claimed that Gorongosa was "ecologically the most diverse park in the world."

*"Are you here to plant trees or help people?"
The answer was "both."*

Gorongosa was established in 1921 as a hunting reserve for the ruling Portuguese—by removing the native people who once had shared the landscape with wildlife.

By 1960, when it was first designated a national park, Gorongosa had become a popular holiday destination for the wealthy. Black Mozambicans, however, were not welcome unless they worked there or were given a special invitation.

After decades of racial inequality, the Marxist Front for the Liberation of Mozambique drove the Portuguese from Mozambique in 1975. But instead of creating a democracy, a brutal single-party socialist government was established. Villagers were forced to relocate into towns or communes. Dissidents were placed in "re-education camps" or convicted in show trials, and many were executed. Within two years, these oppressive measures inspired the formation of the Mozambique Resistance Movement (RENAMO), supported by the governments of South Africa and Rhodesia, which eventually also came

under investigation for severe human rights violations.

The conflict that erupted turned into one of the longest, most brutal, and destructive civil wars in recent decades. Over the course of 15 years (1977–1992), more than 1 million people were killed in the fighting, thousands were tortured, and five million were driven from their homes.

RENAMO established its headquarters near Gorongosa, which, because it is situated near the geographic center of the country, offered a strategic location, plus refuge and food for the rebels.

During the war, wildlife populations declined by 90 to 99%, and continued to decline thereafter partially as a result of post-war poverty. Hungry people needed food, and groups needing cash saw elephant ivory, zebra pelts and others as potential sources of money from the illegal wildlife trade.

A ceasefire halted the war in 1992, but poaching continued, and people in surrounding communities set traps for whatever edible animals remained.

By 1995, the park itself was a dangerous place, not because of the large animals that had been nearly exterminated, but because of landmines.

And by the turn of the century, Gorongosa National Park had effectively been wrecked.

Aerial wildlife counts noted a near total collapse of wildlife. From 1972 to 2001, cape buffaloes declined from 13,000 to 15; wildebeest fell from 6,400 to 1; hippos from 3,500 to 44; zebras from 3,300 to 12; hyenas, black and white rhinos, and wild dogs all fell to 0; and elephants and lions were reduced by 80 to 90%.

Wildlife recovery began in 2008, coinciding with a public and private co-management agreement called the Gorongosa Restoration Project (GRP), a joint partnership between the government of Mozambique and the Carr Foundation, which to this day is still supported by American philanthropist Greg Carr and the government.

At the time, however, the glory of Gorongosa was a memory. Mozambicans told Carr, "Don't bother. There's nothing there anymore."

Carr and the GRP team had a different perspective. They knew the one species crucial to the recovery of the park and its ecosystems—Homo sapiens. The human population surrounding the park was about 250,000, and most subsisted on less than one dollar per day. To be successful in the long run, Gorongosa would have to become more valuable as an intact preserve than as farmland, timberland, and hunting land. It had to embrace the communities that lived around the park and ensure they benefited from the park. When the GRP team was asked by the local community, "Are you here to plant trees or help people?" The answer was "both."

Thus, Gorongosa had to be a "human rights park" as well as a wildlife park, which meant generating tangible benefits for the local people via health care, education, agronomy, and economic development, in addition to protecting its landscape, its waters, and its biological diversity. The goal was to turn what had been a battlefield into a "Park of Peace."

The people living on the mountain were no strangers to hardship. They were doing their best to survive in the face of conflict using traditional methods of farming maize and other low-value crops. This meant they frequently needed new fertile ground and would move up the mountain and cut down the forests.

Recovery was going to take time. Park warden Pedro Muagura, who grew up in the area, remembers in the years following the war, "You used to walk for a day and see perhaps just one warthog."

In 2010, the highlands of Mount Gorongosa (about 3,000 feet) were added to the park, a necessity since the mountain's rainforest receives about 80 inches of rain per year that feeds the rivers winding through the area. Water from the mountain is the lifeblood of the Gorongosa ecosystem.

But across the lower elevations, local people continued cutting, burning, and farming. They had little choice. Feeding one's family will always take precedence over conservation, but this was unsustainable.

Muagura had a radical idea: Why not grow coffee on mountainside plots that had already been deforested? It could be shade-grown, beneath replanted native trees, giving local people an income as well as restoring the forest.

The problem was no one was growing coffee in all of Mozambique. As a member of the restoration team said, "Imagine trying to convince a group of poor farmers who don't know you to plant a crop that they've never heard of, has no nutritional value, and takes three years to start producing."

Nevertheless, park staff, nearly all Mozambicans, taught farmers to care for the delicate coffee plants. In addition to 2,200 coffee plants, 90 hardwood rainforest trees were planted on each hectare that would eventually shade each orchard. To provide the farmers with a living while waiting on returns from the coffee plantation, they also provided seedlings of vegetables like carrots, kale, and peppers, and training in how to grow them.

RENAMO, however, continued as a political and paramilitary organization, and its conflict with the government flared up again in 2013–2014, causing the temporary closure of the park and forcing GRP personnel off the mountain.

And here, finally, Vaida Furanguene, Fatianca Paulino, and Querida Baringuinha, all farmers, enter the scene. The local farmers had embraced the coffee enterprise, but the new plants needed to be watered and the rebels held the top of Mount Gorongosa. No one felt safe going up there in the daylight. So, these women carried water on their heads up the mountain in the dark of night for nearly a year to save the plants.

Because of their efforts, nearly a decade later, more than 600 local farmers are involved in the Gorongosa Project. They're growing arabica coffee under shade trees, simultaneously regenerating the rainforest and generating sustainable income for local agricultural communities.

As of 2022, the park has about 480 acres of farmland, which are reliably producing coffees, with the aim of hitting a total of 2,400 acres by the late 2020s. The hope is to restore nearly 20,000 acres of rainforest around and within the farmland, using coffee production as the catalyst for more regenerative opportunities on the mountain.

Photo courtesy of Gorongosa National Park

Gorongosa coffee bean harvest

And biologically, the coffee forests are bringing the wildlife biodiversity back. Ongoing research projects are proving that only a few years after establishment, these "agroforests" shelter up to 80% of the biodiversity found in the rainforest. By 2018, when the last aerial wildlife survey was conducted, large herbivore populations had recovered by 95%. Gorongosa today is home to at least 100,000 animals.

Illegal hunting and trapping remains an issue, though it has been profoundly curtailed. Over the years, rangers have removed 27,000 snares and traps, and 260 new park rangers (249 men and 11 women) were trained, resulting in increased law enforcement capacity and a 72% decrease in wildlife poaching incidents.

While the reintroduction of some wildlife helped the restoration, 95% of Gorongosa's restoration happened naturally. Nature, when allowed to heal herself, was able to do most of the work on her own.

Equally exciting is the work being done to educate girls. When you educate a girl, you not only get the biggest jump in the socioeconomic status of a community, but also the best chance for long-term success in nature conservation. Women are the fulcrum. Greg Carr notes, "If girls are in school and women have opportunities, then they will have two-child families...This is where human development and conservation merge. Rights for women and children, poverty alleviation—is what Africa needs to save its national parks."

The coffee project's 10-year goal is to be the majority funder of Gorongosa National Park, using business as a sustainable finance mechanism for conservation and human development.

So, buy a bag of coffee from Mozambique (go to *https://ourgorongosa.com* or locally). By doing so, you will help preserve an African equivalent of Yellowstone National Park and support education for girls.

As for the three women at the beginning of this story, it turns out water heroes can be found in a coffee plantation, and Vaida Furanguene, Fatianca Paulino, and Querida Baringuinha are just that.

Photo courtesy of Gorongosa National Park

VICTORIA QUTUUQ BUSCHMAN

Victoria Qutuuq Buschman ~ Alaska, USA

Born in the far northern Iñupiat community of Utqiaġvik in Alaska, Victoria Buschman, the first Inuk Doctor of Conservation Biology in the world, is witnessing firsthand the impacts of climate change. "The Arctic is the most rapidly warming environment in the world and its Indigenous peoples are experiencing unprecedented change. Our homeland is drastically changing at a rate three-to-four times faster than the global average. The things we see, hear, and smell may cease to exist as we know them before the end of this century...For us, the effects of a changing climate are tangible and inescapable even as these processes feel like a distant trouble for the rest of the world. We are living, and breathing, change."

"Standing along the shore, where the Beaufort Sea meets the Chukchi, you can dig the toes of your boots into the cold black sands and stare out beyond the edge of the world."

Located along a gravel spit at 71 degrees north latitude, Utqiaġvik is a small town of perhaps four and a half thousand people, but it is the largest town in a region the size of the United Kingdom. Only 10,000 people live throughout the region, but their heritage dates back thousands of years.

Buschman is a champion for recognizing long-standing Indigenous knowledge and the unique contributions it can bring to Arctic science and governance at all levels.

"My people are definitely ocean people...we have sea ice eight to nine, sometimes even ten months of the year. And this relationship with the ocean completely structures the way that our year occurs. All of our societal organizing is around what is happening on the ocean."

She is currently working as a post-doctoral researcher, jointly staffed at the International Arctic Research Center in Fairbanks, Alaska, and at the Queensland Institute of Natural Resources in Nuuk, Greenland, where she now lives. She works specifically on Indigenous-led wildlife and protected area management, always attempting to partner Indigenous knowledge and science through community-driven research and monitoring.

And sometimes that gets complicated. For example, Utqiaġvik is the largest bowhead whaling community in the world. The community only harvests a few whales a year in very sustainable, traditional ways by sealskin boats called Umiaks. But there's a very strict quota system in the US, which has historically caused policy conflicts. An erroneous study on bowhead whales in 1977 underestimated the population and immediately imposed a conservation ban on Inuit whaling in northern Alaska. When Inuit hunters learned of the ban, they told the scientists they had been observing in the wrong areas, and corrected the mistake by leading the researchers to the whales' preferred habitat.

Buschman notes, "Our entire livelihoods are connected to this particular activity, the whaling seasons. We...cannot sell the meat for money. So, it's only community-based; it's given out to the community after the whale has been caught and there's a big celebration.

"Indigenous relationships to wild living resources are increasingly grounds for establishing new protected areas and developing new policies and practices for partnering wildlife conservation with Indigenous use. This can be controversial as our communities continue to sustainably hunt and fish the charismatic species that have become the global mascots for climate change including seals, whales, walrus, and polar bears. Over decades of gains for Indigenous communities...regarding our rights to sovereignty, co-management, and food security...we are collectively pushing the envelope of what is possible in Arctic conservation efforts.

"One-quarter of all land on earth is owned, managed, used, or occupied by Indigenous peoples, representing 35% of all formal protected areas across the world and 35% of all remaining terrestrial areas experiencing low human impact...As the Arctic warms, it positions Arctic Indigenous communities on the front lines of the most rapidly warming climate in the world. These rapid environmental changes challenge our very livelihoods...food security and cultural continuity.

"We're coming into a period of time where we're finally able to have very nuanced discussions and nuanced understandings of the particular needs, priorities, challenges, and barriers that not only are we facing in the Arctic, but as global societies. How do we come together and tackle some of these issues when we are coming from very different places?

"In my eyes, it's not enough to just do science any more...Indigenous knowledge has a role in shaping research. It has a role in shaping science. It has a role in shaping policy and decision-making, and not just at the local level, but also at the international level. And one of the difficulties is figuring out how do we take all of these different pieces and components at different scales and make it work... Indigenous communities are strong, knowledgeable, and ready to lead conservation efforts."

Photo courtesy of Victoria Buschman

"Our ability to thrive in this mecca of ice, rock, and tundra with below -60°F temperatures is a testament to our knowledge of this environment, the strength of our practices, and the sustainability of our way of life...Here, at the northernmost tip of Alaska, is a landscape few have seen, and still fewer know. This is the home of my people."

Photos courtesy of Victoria Buschman

MARY ALICE McWHINNIE

Mary Alice McWhinnie ~ Illinois, USA

Throughout the first half of the 1900s, the nations that ran Antarctic research programs officially banned women from working there, because they said the rigors of the continent were too great for women. There were also concerns about providing separate bathroom facilities for women, though the real reason, unstated, was fear of sexual misconduct by male researchers.

Only a few women had ever even been to Antarctica at that point. The first woman to set foot on the continent was Caroline Mikkelsen, the wife of a Norwegian whaling captain, who landed with him on the Antarctica peninsula in 1935. In 1937, Ingrid Christiansen, wife of another sea captain, followed her. The first women to winter-over on Antarctica also accompanied their husbands on a private expedition in 1947. And in 1955, Soviet Professor Marie Klenova visited the region as a scientist and helped chart and map the Antarctic coast.

McWhinnie signed off a 1974 letter as, "the girl in the bunny-boots, wind-blown and fishing through 8 feet of sea-ice—at the bottom of the world—the highest, coldest, windiest, most inhospitable place on Earth—Antarctica."

Women were simply personae non gratae in Antarctica. Admiral George Dufek said in 1956 that "women would join American Teams in the Antarctic over his dead body," and that women in Antarctica "would wreck men's illusions of being heroes and frontiersmen."

Women who applied to the British Antarctic Survey (BAS) were likewise discouraged. A letter from BAS personnel sent to a woman who applied in the 1960s read, "Women wouldn't like it in Antarctica as there are no shops and no hairdressers."

Women were still effectively barred from using UK Antarctic bases and logistics until 1987, and women didn't winter-over at the British Halley Research Station until 1996, forty years after the station was established.

The first American Antarctic research station,

McMurdo, was established in 1955 and was little more than a frontier camp. It was located on the bare volcanic rock of Hut Point Peninsula on Ross Island, the solid ground that was both farthest south and accessible by ship. Utilitarian Quonset huts and sheds were scattered here and there, and for the 128 men stationed there, alcohol provided the main social entertainment, so much so that the first few women to visit were protected by military guards.

The first true break for women desiring to work long-term in the Antarctic occurred in 1962 when Dr. Mary Alice McWhinnie, a world authority on krill, sailed for two months on the National Science Foundation's research ship, the USNS *Eltanin*. She was the first American woman to do so, and eventually she completed four additional cruises on the *Eltanin* in 1965, 1967, 1969 and 1970.

Krill are tiny shrimp-like crustaceans that play a key role in Antarctica's food chain. McWhinnie, along with her research assistant, Sister Mary Odile Cahoon, understood the pivotal importance of krill as the primary food source for almost all higher species in the Antarctic—baleen whales, seals, penguins and other birds, fish, and squid.

McWhinnie's pioneering work proved so valuable that in 1972, she was appointed the first-ever female chief scientist on the *Eltanin*, and guided the ship's first venture through the pack ice into Ross Sea.

"*Eltanin* was an ideal research

ship," she said. "I knew that ship for more than ten years—worked on board during six seasons. By the time I left the ship in February 1972, it had the best marine research program in the world. For the first time, marine programs were interacting—exchanging data—studying the entire water column."

Two years later, McWhinnie was asked by the National Science Foundation to become the first woman to winter-over at McMurdo Station where she was eventually appointed chief scientist for the winter Antarctic program, the first female to hold that position.

Then during the 1975-76 summer season, McWhinnie became the first female scientist to work at Palmer Research Station, located on Anvers Island near the Antarctic Peninsula.

Her work included collecting samples through holes drilled in the ice. This enabled her to follow the development and life-cycle of the krill and other species during the sunless winter, which complemented her earlier summer projects conducted on board the research ships. Thanks to her efforts and to her international reputation as one of the foremost krill biologists, Palmer Station became the hub of krill research, and graduate students and researchers from several countries vied for the limited space there to work with her. Research vessels from West Germany, Poland, Argentina and Chile made frequent calls at Palmer Station to enable their scientists to discuss and exchange views with McWhinnnie regarding the biology, distribution and life history of the elusive crustacean.

McWhinnie described the winter isolation in the Antarctic, saying there was not a single bird to be seen, and because of the isolation, the boredom could be extremely challenging for some, though not for her— as she often worked throughout the night in her lab.

Winter came as the last plane flew out at the end of February. Another one wouldn't arrive until the following September. The sun set at 12:45 p.m. in late April, and didn't rise again until August.

Weather, too, posed a safety problem. In July, 1974, 125 mph winds damaged many of the McMurdo buildings, and one support person was found dead in May after having fallen into a 600-foot crevasse.

As women became part of Antarctic exploration and research, cultural change was slow to follow. An article run in Chicago's *The Daily Herald* newspaper in 1974 described women finally coming to Antarctica as integrating the "land with a definite feminine touch." The article discussed women's perfume, ways of entertaining guests and the "dainty feet" of Caroline Mikkelsen.

McWhinnie helped to change that. She became best known for her studies on the krill's distribution, habits, and as a potential food source. Although krill are relatively small—an adult may reach a maximum length just over two inches— their role in the Antarctic ecosystem is crucial. For instance, the yearly southerly migration of baleen whales to Antarctic waters to feed on krill is essential to their survival. The food reserves built up by the whales during their summer krill-feast sustains them throughout most of the rest of the year in more northern waters.

In all, McWhinnie published more than 50 scientific papers, made 11 trips to the Antarctic, and gave numerous presentations on her research findings to other scientists.

McWhinnie developed lung cancer in the fall of 1979, and died in 1980 at the age of 58. At the time of her death, she was an international authority on krill—probably nobody else in the world knew as much about krill as she did. Since her passing, the research center at the Palmer Station was renamed in her honor as the Mary Alice McWhinnie Biology Center, and a mountain peak in the McMurdo chain was named McWhinnie Peak.

Today, McMurdo Station is the logistics hub of the U.S. Antarctic Program. Scientific research is performed at and near McMurdo in astrophysics and geospace sciences, biology and ecosystems, geology and geophysics, glaciology, geomorphology, ice cores, and ocean and climate systems. The station is the largest community in Antarctica, capable of supporting up to 1,200 residents, though only a portion are scientists.

Women are integral members in a wide array of logistical operations, and a part of every scientific discipline, but men still outnumber women in the program nearly two to one. And, as of 2022 in a document released by the NSF, almost three-quarters of women surveyed at Antarctic research stations agreed that sexual harassment was still a problem, describing it as a "fact of life" on the continent.

There's still work to do.

In one letter from 1978, McWhinnie described the conditions aboard her research ship: "I was soaked to the skin and damn near frozen—quiet seas my foot. We were trawling for 7 hours in sea force 5 (all stops at 8) and, as I was sorting animals, we went awash, me included."

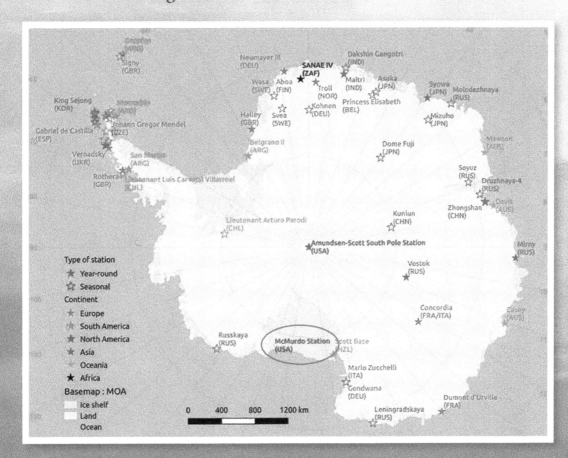

MAIN RESEARCH STATION IN ANTARCTICA

AUNOFO HAVEA FUNAKI

Aunofo Havea Funaki ~ The Kingdom of Tonga

Aunofo Havea Funaki became the first commercially licensed female sea captain in the Kingdom of Tonga and all of Polynesia in 2018. A single mother with five children, Funaki had been sailing for over 30 years, working her way up first cleaning sailing vessels, then working as a cook. When a captain said to her, "You're just the cook. I'm the boss here," it became the catalyst she needed to become a captain herself.

Sailing had long been a solely male endeavor in Polynesia. But in 2000, Funaki was selected to be the only woman amongst a class of 23 students for a maritime course led by the New Zealand Coast Guard. She graduated first in her class.

She now captains many types of vessels, among them vakas, traditional Polynesian canoes, which have been retrofitted to be fossil-free, hybrid transportation systems. These vakas fuse the old with the new, from the use of traditional navigation methods, to natural materials to build the canoes themselves, to solar panels and engines fueled with coconut oil for less pollution.

> *"Saving the oceans is like saving your child—everyone in 100 years will benefit and learn."*

In 2011, Funaki joined the Te Mana O Te Moana (The Spirit of the Ocean) voyage of vakas from New Zealand to Hawaii, the West Coast of the United States, Cocos Island and the Galápagos Islands.

In 2012, she captained an all-women voyage, the first of its kind, through the Tahitian islands to Aitutaki, Cook Island, using only traditional navigation. The women came from across the Pacific: Tonga, Fiji, Samoa, Tahiti, Aotearoa, Hawaii and more.

Sailing a vaka means far more than simply carrying supplies or promoting ecotourism. "Sailing on the vaka across all those miles," says Funaki, "you learn how to voyage relying on the wind, the sun, the stars, your crew and of course, the ocean—the way our ancestors did... There is a sense of connectedness to our people, to the oceans, to nature, to our history and the richness of our cultures and traditions that is such an important part of who we are today. There's also a healing that the ocean gives us; both in terms of its scientific properties, but also on a spiritual level—it keeps us young."

Today, Funaki owns and operates a whale watching company, Vaka & Moana Co., in Vava'u. She is also the founder and Managing Director of the Tonga Voyaging Society, a member of the Okeanos Foundation, which promotes sustainable sea transport, and a passionate advocate of sustainable tourism.

It was a long personal journey, however. One of nine children, Funaki grew up in a time when whales were used for food. In the 1970s, her father was among many who killed whales to feed the communities of Tonga. "I didn't know how to swim in my 20s—I was afraid of the ocean. The fear overcame everything...And I didn't know how important whales were until I was 25."

In 1978, the King of Tonga declared a moratorium on killing whales, and by the 1990s, humpback whales had made enough of a recovery that they were easily seen everywhere around the islands.

Sailing companies soon began offering whale watching trips, and now Funaki takes people whale-watching and swimming with the whales.

Funaki is also a leader in the fight against overfishing and ocean pollution. "Sometimes you see things that are just heartbreaking. Once we saw a whale caught in fishing nets, and there was nothing we could do to untangle it—so we looked on and just cried. It made me realize that sailing on a vaka comes with great responsibility to create more awareness, understanding and respect for each other as human beings and for our oceans."

Plastic pollution, says Funaki, is one of the greatest challenges facing all oceans. "Wherever we were sailing, we would always try to collect whatever rubbish we came across—but there was always more. On our voyage to San Francisco, we saw mounds of plastic debris and nets all meshed together to form a floating island of rubbish."

Of all ocean-related issues, however, climate change looms darkest for vulnerable Pacific islands like Tonga. The Kingdom of Tonga is an archipelago consisting of four clusters of islands. The majority of these islands are comparatively flat except for those raised by tectonic action. Living by the sea is a proud part of Tongan culture and identity, with 80% of the population of 90,000 living right on the coast. Consequently, the effects of climate change, such as increasingly intense tropical cyclones, extreme rainfall events leading to flooding, coastal erosion, heat waves, drought, ocean acidification, and sea level rise pose a profound threat.

For Tongans, who have lived here since the ninth century BCE, the issue of rising sea levels and climate change is not abstract, it's a threat to their very existence. Relocating 90,000 people is not feasible, and if they were to lose their culture, who would Tongans be?

"A lot of people today don't even realize how their actions are a death sentence for our oceans," says Funaki. "Our oceans' health is everyone's responsibility —leaders, communities, youth, everyone—we all must work together in the fight to save our oceans... We are running out of time—the time to act is now. Together we can save our oceans. It's that simple."

Photo courtesy of Christy Butterfield

"Sailing on the vaka across all those miles," says Funaki, "you learn how to voyage relying on the wind, the sun, the stars, your crew and of course, the ocean—the way our ancestors did."

Photos courtesy of Christy Butterfield

TINKER SCHUMAN

Tinker Schuman, Migizikwe, "Eagle Woman"
~ Wisconsin, USA

Tinker and Mary. Photo by John Bates

Mildred "Tinker" Schuman, an Ojibwe elder in the Lac du Flambeau Band of Lake Superior Chippewa of northern Wisconsin, is also known as *Migizikwe*— Eagle Woman. She is deeply respected within the Ojibwe Nation of Lac du Flambeau as a Woman Pipe Carrier, Sweat Lodge Leader, *Ogichida Chidewegon* (Big Drum) Jingle Dress Dancer, and ceremonial Sundancer and Moondancer, as well as a healer, a poet, and an artist.

"In Ojibwe culture, the women are life-givers and guardians of the water...Water is essential for life. It is a gift. It deserves our respect, gratitude and reverence."

Schuman is also a water walker. In recent years, she organized "Water Way Walks" to raise awareness of "Mother Earth's Life Blood—The Water" both for the Lac Du Flambeau community and for the surrounding communities in Vilas County, Wisconsin, a region with one of the highest density of lakes in the world. She said, "I felt like the Creator was nudging me...to energize, honor and pray for Mother Earth's lifeblood, water, which brings healing available to everybody."

The walks began with a sunrise ceremony and a breakfast potluck feast. Then a young girl filled a bucket with water from the Bear River, and the water was passed to Tinker's granddaughter Hattie, then to a teenage girl, then to a mother, then to Schuman, and after that from woman to woman as the 10-mile walk commenced.

"In Ojibwe culture, the women are life-givers and guardians of the water...Water is essential for life. It is a gift. It deserves our respect, gratitude and reverence."

She has dedicated her life to the perpetuation of Anishinaabe culture in all of its aspects—from core spiritual beliefs and customs to songs, dances, regalia and language. Schuman lives her culture and beliefs, inspires others to do so as well, and teaches by example. She has lived through many difficult experiences and has a kind, healing heart that reaches out and embraces others. Her earlier work as an alcohol and drug abuse counselor has helped many people find sobriety, a sense of self-worth, and a cultural pride on the healing path of the Red Road.

She is a great role model for Native women because you can see the Seven Teachings in the way she lives her life.

• Wisdom: As a well-respected elder, she ensures that all are doing things in a way that is grounded in Anishinaabe culture and values. She is a keeper of Anishinaabe oral history and has helped the tribe move forward in a way that honors their history.

• Respect: Schuman is embraced by people of all spiritual faiths because she walks her talk and respects all peoples' spiritual pathways, as well as all living beings.

• Bravery: Schuman is a protector, defender, and provider. As an *Ogichidaakwe* (warrior woman), she stood up for Anishinaabe rights during the very difficult times surrounding the exercise of Native treaty rights when tribal members were harassed, threatened and assaulted for exercising their rights to spear fish in the ceded territory of northern Wisconsin.

• Honesty: She is honest with people without causing harm to the person she is trying to help.

• Humility: Schuman has generously and compassionately supported others without seeking recognition.

• Truth: Schuman speaks her truth, lives her truth, and uses her truth to help others.

• Love: Schuman is spiritually grounded and exudes the kind of peace that one attains when they are clear in their love for the Creator. She loves others with an open heart, and they in turn love her back.

Schuman authored the book *Reborn in the Sun*, co-authored the book *The Healing Blanket*, produced the CD *All My Relatives*, and recently released a book of poetry, *Ba Bii Dwe We Win: Sounds of Living*. She was named Elder of the Year in 2017 by the Wisconsin Indian Education Association.

Schuman had a stroke in 2002 and says of that, "The stroke changed my life quite a bit, but it didn't take my life...At the time, people asked, 'What's going to happen now? What are you going to do?' I told them, 'The Creator has another plan for me.' What we think of as a bad thing might be an opportunity for us to take a different direction in life, or return to the path we were meant to be on...My life has been an amazing journey. I am grateful to have learned from everything that has happened and to be learning still. *Nii Miigwech iwendam.* I am grateful."

WORLD WIDE NIBI-WATER

NIBI, LIKE ONE SACRED DROP BRINGING THE REFRESHMENT
PONDERING THE NEWNESS WHILE CREATING CHANGE.
THE ANCESTORS ARE WATCHING, WHAT WILL I DO?
OUR VOICES GIVE THE PROCLAMATION, OUR VISIBLE ARTS
BRING A TEACHABLE VENUE AS WE TASTE NIBI, HEALING FROM NIBI.
THEN ALL WATER LIFE BEINGS SURVIVE.
THE GREAT SPIRIT HEART IS THE GOOD MEDICINE WITHIN.
FROM ALL PARTS OF THE WORLD IS BEING ACKNOWLEDGED OF THE THIRST
THE DIFFERENT NATIONS NEED FOR SURVIVAL.
THE BLOOD LINE VEIN TRIBUTARIES OF ALL SIZES, LAKES, PONDS,
OCEANS, SEAS ARE THE BLESSINGS OF THE SPIRIT, FOR OUR
OFFSPRINGS DECENDENTS FOR GENERATIONS TO COME.
THIS MOTHER EARTH,
WORLD WIDE WOMEN SHARING THEIR LIFE AND PROTECTION AS LIFE
GIVERS, BEING THE LEADERS TO BRING AWARENESS.
WAKE UP, FIGHT THE POLLUTION, SAVE THE FAMILIES, SING YOUR
SONGS, SAY YOUR HUMBLE PRAYERS, THE MIGHTY SPIRITUAL WINDS
RISE! RISE! RISE! RISE! RISE! RISE! RISE!

MIGIZIKWE NINDIZHINIKAZ
November 17, 2022

Photo by John Bates

"I felt like the Creator was nudging me...to energize, honor and pray for Mother Earth's lifeblood, water, which brings healing available to everybody."

Photo by Misty Jackson

Photo by John Bates

TĀWERA TAHURI

Tāwera Tahuri ~ New Zealand

Ko au te wai, ko te wai ko au: "I am the water and the water is me." The saying is a *Te Reo Māori* (Māori Language) expression frequently used to state the deep Māori relationship with *Kaupapa Moana* (Ocean), *Kaupapa Wai Māori* (Fresh Water) and *Kaupapa Awa* (Rivers). Rivers and lakes are integral to Māori cultural identity. Water is understood to be the essence of all life, akin to the blood of *Papatuanuuku* (Earth mother) who supports all people, plants and wildlife.

Tāwera Tahuri, a multidisciplinary artist, teacher and activist born in Raetihi, New Zealand, and affiliated with the Ngā Ariki Kaipūtahi, Whakatōhea, Ngāti Uenuku, and Tūwharetoa Māori tribes, is passionate about freshwater ways. She is actively involved in the care and maintenance of sacred waterways and takes her role as a *kaitiaki* or guardian seriously.

Tahuri is actively involved in the care and maintenance of sacred waterways and takes her role as a kaitiaki or guardian seriously.

As a board member for The Seventh Generation Fund for Indigenous Peoples, the first international board representative and Māori voice for the US-based Indigenous organization, Tahuri is committed to Indigenous issues across the world and proudly represents her peoples alongside her wider Indigenous family.

The Treaty of Waitangi, signed in 1840, has been the basis for her recent bodies of work. The Treaty was written in English and translated into Māori. Some words in the English treaty did not translate directly into the written Māori of the time. In the English version, Māori ceded the sovereignty of New Zealand to Britain and gave the Crown the exclusive right to purchase lands they wished to sell. In return, Māori were guaranteed full ownership of their lands, forests, fisheries and other possessions and were given the rights of British subjects.

However, in the Māori language version of the Treaty, the word *sovereignty* was translated as *kawanatanga* ("governance"). And in contradiction to the English language version, Māori retained authority and sovereignty, and did not give this to the Queen.

Māori have challenged breaches of the treaty since shortly after its signing in 1840. In 1975 the Treaty of Waitangi Act established the Waitangi Tribunal to hear claims of Crown violations of the Treaty of Waitangi. For example, The Waikato-Tainui Raupatu Claims (Waikato River) Settlement Act 2010 provides redress through a new co-governance entity to oversee the management of the river that will protect its health and wellbeing for present and future generations.

Tahuri writes, "The Seventh Generation principle serves not only as a reminder of the wrongs of the past but also the hopes and aspirations of the future seven generations."

For one of her exhibits, Tahuri has made crosses in the shape of the signatures made by the Maori chiefs on the 1840 Treaty of Waitangi.

She has traveled extensively as an artist and regularly represents Indigenous Māori Artists on an international stage. She has produced a prolific amount of work throughout her artistic career and is actively involved in her community as a teacher and performer.

Ko au te wai, ko te wai ko au:
"I am the water and the water is me."

Photo courtesy of Tāwera Tahuri

Photos courtesy of Tāwera Tahuri

Tāwera Tahuri with Grandmother Josephine Mandamin-Ba

MONICA LEWIS-PATRICK

Monica Lewis-Patrick ~ Michigan, USA

When Michigan declared bankruptcy in 2014 on behalf of the city of Detroit, nearly a third of its debt was $5.7 billion owed to the city by its own water department. As an austerity measure, the department began shutting off water for residents who were more than $150 behind on their water bills, initiating a massive water shutoff campaign. Since then, an estimated 100,000 households have been disconnected from water and sanitation services.

How did this happen? In a city where nearly 40 percent of its people live in poverty, water had become increasingly unaffordable for many of its residents. The cost of water had risen about 96 percent in eight years prior to 2014. The average Detroiter was paying 20 percent of their pretax income on water, a number nearly 10 times as high as the EPA recommended 2.5 percent of household income. A United Nations rights expert who reviewed the situation said, "It is contrary to human rights to disconnect water from people who simply do not have the means to pay their bills."

"My grandmother called it making a way out of no way," she says. "You stay in the room till you get what you came for."

Not only did families have their water shut off, they also lived under the threat of a visit from social services, because the agency can take children out of homes that don't have water for more than 72 hours. Not long after, in 2015, banks foreclosed on 14,000 homes based on water debt alone.

Enter Monica Lewis-Patrick, one of the founders of We the People of Detroit (WTPD), an organization begun in 2009 to educate and empower Detroit residents on important civil rights issues, including water access. Now President and CEO of WTPD, Lewis-Patrick jumped deep into the water fray when she learned that the City of Detroit had cut off the water of an apartment building occupied by mothers and senior citizens. She was particularly incensed that more than 84% of North America's freshwater comes from the Great Lakes, yet "many minority and low-income communities near the Great Lakes and throughout the U.S. do not have access to clean water."

WTPD took action. In one year, the WTPD team and Lewis-Patrick—who soon became known throughout the environmental justice community as the "Water Warrior"—were able to save 800 homes from water debt foreclosure. They continue to this day giving low-income families access to clean water; providing education on water issues; conducting research to raise awareness; and mobilizing people to take action. WTPD also manages a water rights hotline so people can get emergency assistance, and oversees four water stations that deliver water directly to those in need if they cannot make it to a station.

Lewis-Patrick first took up a civil rights cause when she was 12. She urged her Tennessee hometown school board not to remove Black literature from the curriculum. "In my small town, the African American population was less that 2%, but I wanted to take that class." She and a few friends organized students to resist the school board's decision—and they won. "That was the first time I was able to change policy," she says. And from then on, "I don't remember not being in some kind of organizing, mobilizing movement," she says.

"[Water access] is a daily struggle and part of that struggle is there's not enough information about water access ...On top of that storm, there's little empathy and compassion for [low-income] persons, so some of the work that we've done is to bring more validity to the voice of the communities impacted by the water shut-offs."

Lewis-Patrick says the goal of WTPD and the Great Lakes Water Quality Advisory Board is to create a pathway towards access to clean, safe and affordable water for all. Her passionate advocacy helps to make her exceptionally effective. "My grandmother called it making a way out of no way," she says. "You stay in the room till you get what you came for."

Staying in the room has led Lewis-Patrick to be an active member of the Michigan Water Unity Table, Michigan State University (MSU) Water Fellows, the University of Michigan's Water Center's Lead & Copper Rule Committee, US Human Rights Network and the Healing Our Waters (HOW) Equity Advisory Action Council. In October 2014, she co-hosted the United Nations Rapporteurs on Water/Sanitation and Housing. There she challenged the U.N.'s Human Right to Water and Sanitation, as clean, safe and affordable water was being denied to Detroit residents.

She is a co-author of the 2016 book *Mapping the Water Crisis: The Dismantling of African-American Neighborhoods in Detroit*, which documents the effects of political and economic policies and their relationship to race in Detroit.

In 2019 she was appointed to the International Joint Commission (IJC) Great Lakes Water Quality Advisory Board, and she received an appointment to the Michigan Advisory Council on Environmental Justice by Governor Gretchen Whitmer.

She has built a legacy of accomplishments, but the fight is never ending. "As my mother said, nobody gives you equity and justice. You have to bring equity and justice on your two legs, in every room you enter. And one thing is sure about Black women, we love all of our children, unapologetically and unconditionally. That means we love all of humanity enough to tell them the truth and enough to advocate that everyone has a pathway to clean, safe, affordable water, air, and a world that considers their best interests."

This is, of course, not only a Detroit issue. Water security—having access to sufficient quantities of safe water in people's daily lives—is at great risk with emerging classes of water "haves" and "have-nots" around the world. The shifting patterns of water availability, along with falling groundwater levels, now limits and will further limit access to drinking water and water for irrigation, presenting new socio-economic and political implications. Over 2 billion people already lack access to safe drinking water at home, and by 2025

over half of the world's population will reside in water-stressed areas. These numbers will continue to increase if climate change and population growth follow predicted trajectories. Is the world prepared for waves of displaced people? Millions of people are forecast to become water refugees. How will their migration to water-secure places be managed? Are neighboring countries willing and prepared to accept these displaced populations?

Lewis-Patrick's tireless work is at the heart of confronting a world-wide problem, which requires a joining of all people, all forces. She has spoken about the United Nations Resolution that water and sanitation are basic human rights. But sometimes the fight comes down locally to one community at a time. "I sat at the knee of some of the greatest minds and some of the greatest women that have held down policy and education and human rights in this city," she recalls. "We're committed to building transformative work that our young people can build off. There's always some struggle but we don't have to have the same struggles. We don't have to just accept that things are just bad. We have the opportunity to really make this an equitable and compassionate and fair community we all can live in."

"We didn't call ourselves into this fight. We tell folks that we didn't choose water. Water chose us. In the divinity of water, water was before everything else was. We see ourselves as called into this great layer of warrior women that are fighting for water all around the globe, from Cochabamba to the Arab Spring, from Ireland to the Navajo Nation, from all over these Great Lakes where we have what I call 'bad revolutionary sisters' who have decided that not only will *they* drink, but that their children's children's children will drink. Our vision is even deeper than what we can see right now. It's a transformative way of thinking."

"*In the divinity of water, water was before everything else was. We see ourselves as called into this great layer of warrior women that are fighting for water all around the globe.*"

Photos courtesy of Monica Lewis-Patrick/We the People of Detroit

ALETA BAUN

Photos courtesy of Goldman Environmental Prize

Aleta Baun, an Indigenous leader from West Timor on Timor Island in Indonesia, won the prestigious Goldman Environmental Prize in 2013 for helping to stop the destruction of sacred mountains and forest lands that protect the headwaters of West Timor's major rivers. Baun lives in the Mollo region of West Timor at the foot of the Mutis mountain range. Mutis means "the flow of water."

In the 1990s, the district government issued illegal permits to mining companies to cut marble from the mountains in Mollo territory. As mining began, deforestation and landslides became commonplace, water in wellsprings diminished and became polluted, and many springs disappeared altogether. Villagers were forced to move from their traditional land without compensation. The cut marble was destined for floors and kitchen tops in the US, China, Singapore, Korea and Japan.

> *"We want to empower women who fight. We want to tell them there will be challenges in every struggle, but what is important is they should not be afraid because if our environment is destroyed, it is women who suffer the most."*

The mining quickly became a profound threat to the Mollo people's rights to their territory and to their survival. The Mollo people are believed to have occupied the land around the mountain range for 13,000 years. They consider the soil, water, stones and trees to be part of themselves—the land symbolizes the flesh, the water blood, the stones bones, and forests veins and hair. The stones are believed to form the backbone of the Mollo people. In Mollo tradition, mining marble would be like leaving a person without a spine.

Baun explains, "If we are separated from any one of these natural elements, or if any one of the elements are destroyed, we start to die and lose our identity."

Baun saw that the only way to stop the mining "was to go from house to house and village to village and reach as many people as possible with our message." Over many months, Baun and three other women met with the local people from the 22 villages in the Mollo territory. They discussed the history of the stone, the history of the region, and the environmental and social impacts the mining would bring to their community.

And in June 2000, they succeeded in stopping the mining.

But that same year, a Jakarta-based company was issued a thirty-year permit to operate another mine on other rock outcrops, including Fatu Nausus, a sacred mountain to the Mollo. The company promised to build houses, power plants, a school, a health clinic, and a church, as well as improve the roads for the local community. Their promises lead to factions forming between villagers, and Baun took to organizing under the cover of night.

As told in Mollo tradition, "The mountain didn't always exist. According to legend, three women on a journey once took shelter here to breastfeed their children. The women turned into the mountain, and it became known as Nausus. The word Nausus means 'to embrace and nurse'. So this mountain is called 'the breastfeeding mountain.'"

The story is rich in symbolism, because these mountains protect the headwaters of thirteen rivers across West Timor, which supply drinking and irrigation water for much of the region. "There's no mountain here without a spring," Baun notes. "They have pores underneath them, which act as water reservoirs."

The rivers, in turn, bring water to the people, irrigate their lands, and nurture them.

So when mining came to Fatu Nausus, people came together not only to protect their water, but to defend Mother Earth.

Baun warned community leaders of the negative impacts of the mine. "It's true you have money now, but you should remember that your name came from the rocks, from the trees." Timorese surnames are traditionally derived from sacred local rocks, waters, or forests, professing their bearers as guardians of the elements of nature after which their clan are named.

New mines continued to open despite the renewed local opposition. Sixty-two acres of farmland were cleared in an area that was a crucial food source for the community. Landslides became increasingly common again, and rivers became contaminated. Drought periods intensified as well springs disappeared.

Baun continued to organize resistance, and hundreds of villagers joined her. They demanded that the District Head and the regional parliament cancel the mine, but they were denied.

Baun realized that the women had to do more. They decided to bring their looms to the mining site and stay as long as it took, all while weaving traditional tenun cloth.

Baun later said in an interview, "Women are the recognized landowners in the Mollo culture, and this reawakened in those women who hadn't been actively speaking out a desire to protect their land. Women decided to stage a sit-in at the mining site, weaving their colorful intricate tapestries in a show of resilience and protest of the mine...Weaving brought them strength, using dyes sourced from the forests, cotton from forest cotton vines, to create vibrantly colored patterns and symbols of their tribal totems, deeply linked to their homelands."

Their weaving was a symbolic act. One of the protesters later said that they were weaving the cloth to metaphorically "wrap it around the marble. As if the marble field is a ball, we wanted to show that it belonged to us by working hard wrapping it. We wanted to show them that the land belongs to the people, regardless if we're still alive or dead."

The men showed their support by taking on domestic duties at home.

The mining companies retaliated by hiring thugs and targeting the women with violence.

One night on her way home, Baun was surrounded by thirty men who discussed whether to rape or kill her. Instead, they took her money, hacked her legs with machetes and rammed her head into a tree, leaving deep scars that remain today.

Fearing for her life, Baun took her two-month-old baby and went into hiding in the forests around Mollo. For six months she moved from village to village to escape the security forces paid for by the mining company who had put a price on her head. The village communities protected and sheltered her.

The violence failed. Instead of frightening the women off, the attacks reinforced their resistance.

By 2006, 150 women occupied the mine site, and for nearly a year, they demonstrated peacefully, continuing to weave their traditional cloth. Others helped by keeping track of police and security forces. The campaign caught media attention domestically and internationally, and the pressure on the mining companies mounted.

By 2007, the mining companies ceased activity at the site.

Eventually all mining within the Mollo territories was abandoned in 2010, and Indonesian government officials returned the mined land to the traditional Mollo landowners.

Baun dedicated funds from the Goldman Environmental Prize to Organisasi A'Taimamus, which supports sustainable farming and other income-generating activities in the Mollo region, including empowering women through weaving enterprises, and providing legal advocacy and a credit union.

In 2014, Baun was elected to the provincial parliament, one of only five women out of 65 members. During this time, in addition to raising three children, Baun also completed a law degree.

Baun now works with communities across West Timor to map their traditional forests as a preemptive strategy to establish indigenous territorial rights. Indonesia is home to about 70 million indigenous people, many of whom do not have formal title to the land that their families have lived on for generations. Without help, they have little protection when developers try to move into their homeland.

New challenges loom with the increasing unpredictability of rains due to climate change.

But Baun notes that the years of struggle have increased the ability of Mollo's people to control their fate. "What's interesting to me is that the Indigenous peoples' knowledge has been strengthened, of philosophies that are deeply related to nature. This enables people to make informed decisions. Nature is a vast library, and there's a unique way for us to learn from it."

Baun has one final rule for anyone wishing to do business on West Timor: "Lands and forests cannot be destroyed, stones cannot disappear, and water cannot be dried up."

Photos courtesy of Goldman Environmental Prize

"We don't deny that we are behind in terms of electricity, infrastructure, and all those amenities of development. But we do not need to live in excess. That will only cause us to forget who we are, forget unity, and forget our community. We prefer to live in modesty."

AUTUMN PELTIER

Autumn Peltier ~ Ontario, Canada

In 2018, at the age of thirteen, Autumn Peltier stood before the United Nations General Assembly in New York City and spoke about the importance of protecting water.

Born in 2004, Peltier first became interested in water protection when she was eight years old and her mother took her to a water ceremony in Serpent River First Nation, Ontario. She saw signs all over the walls that read "Not for Consumption," or "Do not use for handwashing," or "Boil water advisory." Later, she did her own research and discovered that many First Nations Communities in Ontario had been on boil-water advisories for years. She knew Canada was a water-rich country, and wondered why so many native people had broken pipelines and mine wastes that contaminated their water.

"Water is a basic human right. Everyone deserves access to clean drinking water, no matter what our race or color is, or how rich or poor we are."

Peltier grew up on Manitoulin Island on Lake Huron in Ontario as a member of the Wikwemikong First Nation. Her mentor on water rights was her great-aunt, Grandmother Josephine Mandamin-Ba, one of the first to lead water walks throughout the Great Lakes and Canada. When asked the best advice she received from Grandmother Josephine-Ba, Peltier says, "It's actually what she told me the day before she passed away. 'People are going to try to stop you, but you just have to keep on doing the work and keep on loving the water'...Carrying on her legacy is one of the most important things to me."

In 2016, she met with Prime Minister Justin Trudeau where, in tears, she insisted he do the right thing and prevent further water pollution from additional pipeline projects that he had endorsed, all of which would endanger First Nation communities.

She addressed the United Nations Global Landscapes Conference in September 2019 and said, "It all started by learning why my people couldn't drink the water on Ontario Indigenous lands. I was confused because Canada is not a third-world country, but in my country, the Indigenous people live in third-world conditions...For years and years, our ancestors have passed down traditional oral knowledge that our water is alive and our water has a spirit. Our first water teaching comes from our mother. We literally live in water for nine months, floating in that sacred water that gives us life."

She was also appointed the Chief Water Commissioner for the Anishinabek Nation in 2019, which means she speaks on behalf of 40 First Nations in Ontario. She has called for a banning of plastics and a return to older, more sustainable ways of life. "We can't eat money or drink oil."

Peltier says, "My people believe this to be true [that water is alive and has a spirit]. Our water deserves to be treated as human with human rights. We need to acknowledge our waters with personhood so we can protect our waters."

As a teenager, Peltier has already made enormous strides for clean water not only in indigenous communities, but throughout Canada and the United States.

She is an extraordinary inspiration to young people, in particular to Native youth, though there's an immense amount of work she still wants to do. "Everyone listens but nothing changes," she has said. "It's young people, people who are sixteen today, who are changing and who have really internalized the environmental challenge.

"No one should have to worry if

the water is clean or if they will run out of water. No child should grow up not knowing what clean water is or never know what running water is. One day I will be an ancestor, and I want my great-grandchildren to know I tried hard to fight so they can have clean drinking water."

Peltier earned the title of Water Warrior years ago. Peltier's documentary movie *The Water Walker*, produced by Seeing Red Six Nations, was released on HBO Canada in 2021. She's already received many awards, including in 2021, when she was one of three winners for the International Planetary Health Awards, recognizing Advocacy and Achievement in Water, Biodiversity and Climate Change.

She has been shortlisted for the International Children's Peace Prize three times, and in 2022 was runner-up for International Children's Peace Prize with the Nobel Peace Prize committee. That same year, she earned the Emerging Leader of Canada Award from the Public Policy Forum of Canada.

Her best advice to other young women is to "keep going, don't look back, and if you have an idea, just do it; no one is going to wait for you or tell you what to do. Use your voice and speak up for our planet."

She plans to "keep meeting other youth with the same passion, and help inspire Nations of youth to stand up for our future and our great grandchildren's future. I also hope to visit places where the water is considered sacred and meet the ones who understand the sacredness of water."

Peltier travels all over the world now, advocating for clean water. "Water is a basic human right. Everyone deserves access to clean drinking water, no matter what our race or color is, or how rich or poor we are."

Photo courtesy of Stephanie Peltier, photo by Linda Roy

Photo by Jessica Deeks via Seeing Red Media

Photo courtesy of Stephanie Peltier, photo by Linda Roy

Photo courtesy of Stephanie Peltier, photo by Linda Roy

"We can't eat money or drink oil...keep going, don't look back, and if you have an idea, just do it; no one is going to wait for you or tell you what to do. Use your voice and speak up for our planet."

MARINA RIKHVANOVA

Marina Rikhvanova ~ Russia

At 5,400 feet deep and 25 million years old, Lake Baikal is the deepest and oldest lake in the world. A United Nations World Heritage Site, it rests in a narrow rift valley at the southern edge of Siberia near the Mongolian border, and stretches for 395 miles. The lake holds 22% of all the freshwater worldwide, more water than all of North America's Great Lakes combined, and it's home to more than 1,600 species of plants and animals, 800 of which are endemic. Known as the Galapagos of Russia, its age, isolation, and cold, oxygen-rich waters have produced one of the world's richest and most unusual freshwater faunas. One unique species is the golomyanka, a pink, partly transparent fish which gives birth to live young. Another is the Nerpa or Baikal seal, the only exclusively freshwater seal species in the world. Scientists are still bewildered by this species given that the lake is landlocked and located hundreds of miles away from the ocean.

Photos courtesy of Goldman Environmental Prize

"Baikal is an indicator of whether modern man can curb his appetite and preserve what nature has created. It's a kind of red line for humanity."

Marina Rikhvanova grew up visiting the shores of Lake Baikal and fell in love with the lake. Later, when she trained as a biologist at the university in Irkutsk, she studied the Baikal Pulp and Paper Mill that was built right on the shores of the lake in 1966. Through her research, Rikhvanova learned that the mill was dumping up to 200,000 cubic meters of liquid waste per day into the lake. The pollution was killing the lake's unique wildlife, and women in the surrounding communities were experiencing a high rate of perinatal mortality and miscarriage. In addition, air pollution created a constant putrid smell, and local people were dying from lung diseases at a rate two times the national average.

The chemical pollutants discharged by the mill were also turning up in the milk of the Nerpa seals.

A mother of two, Rikhvanova decided to devote her life to saving the lake.

In the early 1990s, she helped to found the Baikal Environmental Wave, which soon began organizing demonstrations, petition-signings, and community meetings, all aimed at bringing an end to the mill's pollution of Baikal.

The group monitored the illegally dumped effluents, and though there was mounting political pressure to stop, they continued to protest. By the mid-2000s, Baikal Wave grew to an organization of twenty-one multiethnic employees and many volunteers, supported with local and international funding.

In the midst of these protests in 2002, the Russian government announced plans to build the longest petroleum pipeline in the world, extending 2,566 miles from eastern Siberia to an oil terminal on Russia's Pacific coast, right through the Lake Baikal basin. Transneft, Russia's state-owned oil company, proposed building the pipeline within a half-mile of Lake Baikal, despite concerns about possible oil spills and leakage. Rikhvanova opposed the plan and embarked on a many-year struggle to divert the pipeline.

Working within Russia's increasingly repressive climate, Rikhvanova successfully led a national campaign that included rallying thousands in protest and obtaining over 200,000 signatures to stop the pipeline. Due to these efforts, in

April 2006, President Vladimir Putin ordered the pipeline to be rerouted away from the lake's watershed, marking a tremendous success for civil society and the environmental movement in Russia.

However, the Wave paid a political price. After 2000, the organization experienced continual official monitoring and harassment, including periodic office raids and computer confiscation. Particularly dramatic was a night raid in 2007 by fifteen masked men wielding iron bars and shouting Russian nationalist slogans. They invaded and wrecked an environmentalist camp that Rikhvanova had helped to organize. One person was killed, and five seriously injured. Many environmentalists were arrested, among them Rikhvanova's son, allegedly framed as one of the brawlers. The authorities held him for a year before releasing him. "That was a terrible year for us," Rikhvanova said.

In 2008, Rikhvanova was the recipient of a Goldman Environmental Prize which recognizes individuals for sustained and significant efforts to protect and enhance the natural environment, often at great personal risk.

That same year, the paper mill closed, not due to the protests, but because of its economic unprofitability.

Nevertheless, in 2010, Russian Prime Minister Vladimir Putin decided to restart it.

And again, Rikhvanova led protests. In an interview, she said, "Scientists have come to the conclusion that if this is to continue another 10 years, Baikal's endemic species could disappear altogether."

In a later interview, she noted, "After the mill's closure in October 2008, the factory laid off the majority of its 2,000 workers, which caused tensions in the town of Baikalsk as workers demanded their unpaid wages and unemployment benefits.

"Then, on January 13th [2010], Russian Prime Minister Putin signed a decree amending the list of banned activities on Baikal, allowing the production of cellulose on the lake's shores without the requirement of a closed wastewater system...

"Many locals consider the enormous lake, the 'Pearl of Siberia,' sacred, and a national pride and treasure. Seeing it put at risk again caused more than 1,500 people to protest on the streets of Irkutsk one month after Putin signed his decree."

In 2011, Rikhvanova waded into snow up to her chest to discover and photograph the mill's illegal dumping of lignin-based slurry, an industrial waste product. Her group's report to UNESCO played a crucial role in closing the mill, this time in 2013. But ecological reasons hardly drove the decision. The mill amassed debts, and the business was deemed unviable.

Despite the clear and continued risks of the mill's pollution, there was a lot of local pushback to closing it. The Baikal Pulp and Paper Mill generated 80 percent of Baikalsk's income. When the plant closed again, more than 1,500 people lost their jobs.

Rikhvanova and her colleagues took this as an opportunity. They sketched out a plan to make Baikalsk eco-friendly, and started a school for eco-business, teaching residents alternative ways to make a living through eco-tourism and other sustainable livelihoods.

Rikhvanova used funds from an environmental prize to subsidize nine projects submitted to a contest she sponsored for residents to create environmentally friendly jobs.

By 2013, government pressure escalated as it attempted to designate the Baikal Environmental Wave as a "foreign agent" due to its support from international organizations. The law was enacted as a way for the Russian government to further repress civil society groups. The group fought this in the courts, but in 2016, the Baikal Environmental Wave was classified as a foreign agent, and liquidated.

Now the fight to save the lake has shifted to another battleground—unmanaged tourism. Baikal has become Russia's biggest tourism sensation, especially among travelers from Asia, with visitor numbers growing to over 2 million. But most areas lack centralized sewage and treatment facilities necessary to cope with mass tourism.

One of the major concerns with increasing tourism is that a decade ago, scientists discovered Spirogyra, a kind of algae that is not typically found in Baikal, growing next to some of the most popular tourist spots and spreading fast. In just a few years, spirogyra covered most of the lake's bed near touristed places, prompting the experts to conclude its appearance was a direct result of unfiltered sewage being dumped from new properties.

In 2023, environmental protesters in Russia risk immediate arrest. Where Baikal's ecological future is going appears equally at risk.

"As a biology student at the University of Irkutsk, I monitored the damaging human impact on the lake. I realized how fragile this magnificent lake was. Baikal has been around for 25 million years, yet human beings could destroy it so quickly."

"When you see results from your work, you want to continue. You have to persevere."

Photos courtesy of Goldman Environmental Prize

GRETCHEN GERRISH

Gretchen Gerrish ~ Wisconsin, USA

Since Gretchen Gerrish was a doctoral student nearly two decades ago, she has been traveling to Belize to study bioluminescent shrimp-like crustaceans called marine ostracods. These tiny creatures (less than a millimeter to a few millimeters long) live in the shallow waters of the Caribbean Sea and create phantasmagorical light displays in the dark water. They use their light to attract mates, but also to surprise and deter predators. They even continue to emit light when swallowed, causing predators to spit them out in order to avoid lighting themselves up and being easily spotted by their own predators.

Photo courtesy of Gretchen Gerrish

"I love that we face completely new and unknown discoveries on a regular basis."

In some ostracod species, like *P. annecohenae*, bioluminescence is also used for courtship displays, much like fireflies on land. Males of each species employ distinct patterns of light pulses (seen as a string of dots) that attract only females of the same species. Like a Fourth of July fireworks display, the courtship display is performed in absolute darkness in order for the males to have the best chance of being spotted by females. The males initially emit short bursts of bright blue light in a sort of dance that lasts an average of 45 minutes, and then as they spiral vertically up the water column, they create more flashes of light that are less bright.

Called "blue sand" or "blue tears" because they are so tiny, these ostracods produce chemical compounds in a special gland called "the light organ." Gathered in a mass, their collective bioluminescence is bright enough that Japanese soldiers during World War II used them as a light to read by at night, but one not bright enough to give away their position to enemies.

Remarkably, most of the animals in our oceans make light! Gretchen Gerrish studies a suite of approximately 65 different bioluminescent ostracod species, of which only about 20 are currently described. She notes that "a lot of our work has been done on *P. annecohenae* because it is one of the easiest to collect.

Most species can only be collected by sweeping a net through their luminescent displays, which means we can only find adult males and occasional females for most species. We don't know what most species eat or where they live.

"There is still a lot to discover about luminescent ostracods. Every Caribbean site we visit, we discover six to eight new species. We do not fully understand their ecological association with the ocean environment. But, their high densities and known scavenging behaviors suggest that they may function much like ants in a forest, cleaning up decaying creatures and waste constantly produced in coral reef environments.

"I love that we face completely new and unknown discoveries on a regular basis. Finding new species is still a thrill. Discovery of new multispecies synchronized behaviors, building the family tree, understanding how they see, and even figuring out something as simple as what a species eats or what kind of parasites it has are intriguing. It is amazing to apply existing scientific knowledge to make predictions for this unique system and then to reject and revise those ideas as we learn!"

Her research has been funded by the National Science Foundation since 2014, and was featured in David Attenborough's documentary "Light on Earth" and in the BBC version, "Life That Glows."

Back home in the Midwestern United States, Gerrish's research also includes studying evolutionary ecology in aquatic invertebrates. She is currently studying zooplankton community changes occurring in the Mississippi River in response to the invasion of Asian Carp.

She is also the director of the University of Wisconsin-Trout Lake Station, a northern Wisconsin field station world-renowned for its research that began in 1926. "It requires persistent and dedicated effort to sustain a truly continuous data set," she says. The Trout Lake Station was named the North Temperate Lakes Long-Term Ecological Research site in 1981, "and is used by people all over the world to ask climate and lake-dynamic questions."

Besides coordinating a host of field studies at the station, she is also personally working on the effects of climate change on lake dwelling creatures which are experiencing more variable and extreme spring conditions. And she collaborates with other researchers to look at the decline in northern stands of wild rice in order to understand what influences the recovery and success of future rice populations.

"Natural history and discovery matter. We should strive to learn about and from the natural world. Evolution is not a straight or fully understood path."

She also loves working with the dozens of students who, besides the permanent science staff, conduct research every summer at the station. "Co-learning and working side-by-side with students is intrinsic to all aspects of my research. It is through their fresh eyes and exploration that innovative thoughts and initiatives solidify into discovery."

Photo by Anita Gerrish

"Co-learning and working side-by-side with students is intrinsic to all aspects of my research. It is through their fresh eyes and exploration that innovative thoughts and initiatives solidify into discovery."

Photo courtesy of Gretchen Gerrish

Photo by Anita Gerrish

RUTH BUENDÍA

Ruth Buendía ~ Peru

A member of the Asháninka tribe of Peru, the largest Indigenous group in the Peruvian Amazon, Ruth Buendía was 12 years old in 1989 when her father was assassinated, along with thousands more, by "Shining Path" guerrillas. The guerillas, a Maoist revolutionary group, had invaded their lands in the mid-1980s. Shining Path took Buendía, her mother, and her four younger siblings to a camp built in the Ene River valley where they were held captive, forced to work the land, and made to give up their language and speak Quechua or Spanish. Those who rebelled were stabbed or hung in front of their families. (According to the final report by the Truth and Reconciliation Commission, more than 30 Asháninka communities disappeared, some 10,000 natives were displaced, 5,000 were kidnapped and 6,000 were killed.)

"On my back, I carry my culture, my territory, my family, and my ancestors that came before me, which I need to defend."

A year later, Buendía convinced her mother, now skin and bones from malaria, to flee into the forest to the Ene river. She helped her mother into a basket that Asháninka women use to carry yucca, and she carried her mother down to the river on her back.

Photos courtesy of Goldman Environmental Prize

They were rescued by the Asháninka army who have a reputation for being the strongest warriors—the best with a bow and arrow—of the 65 Amazonian tribes in Peru.

Though now safe, her mother couldn't support her, so Buendía was sent to Lima to work as a maid for a family of evangelicals. At 17 years old, she returned to Satipo, Peru, where she worked as a cook and server while she finished school and raised her first daughter alone.

At 21, a client invited her to join CARE, an organization that defends the rights and land of the Asháninkas. Traveling along the Ene River, Buendía ran

Photos courtesy of Goldman Environmental Prize

into Asháninka leaders who had known and respected her father. She felt at home again and became trusted.

In 2005, when the president of CARE resigned from his post, she entered the election—the first time an Asháninka woman had dared to run as a candidate for president. And she won! Ene River valley communities have only male chiefs, and Ruth Buendía became the representative of all of them.

Economic terrorism followed the civil war. The ancestral home of the Asháninka in Peru's Ene River valley came under siege by a never-ending list of exploitative industries looking to clear the rainforest, mine for gold, drill for oil, and dam rivers.

In 2008, the Peruvian government authorized the construction of a 65-meter-tall concrete hydroelectric dam in the Ene River canyon, and gave it the name Pakitzapango, the "House of the Eagle," from the creation myth where the feathers of the eagle became all the Amazon people who were yet to be born.

The project promised enough power to provide electric lighting for almost 800,000 homes. Not only would

Peruvians get cheaper electricity, but the Brazilians would buy the surplus over 30 years, creating more "growth" for the natives.

Ruth Buendía did not believe it. She brought in a team of engineers in 2010 to corroborate what was suspected: The artificial lake created by the dam was going to flood more than 700 square kilometers of jungle. Ten indigenous communities would lose 65 percent of their cropland and would be forced to higher reaches of the jungle.

"First terrorism displaced us. Now they are going to build dams to displace us again." For Buendía, this was also terrorism—this time by investors.

However, the Peruvian government never asked the Asháninkas if they agreed with the plan despite a prior consultation law requiring the government to consult with Indigenous communities before launching development projects that will affect them.

"It's as if the government went into your home without asking and said: 'Sir, we have found oil under your land. So leave, please, it belongs to all Peruvians.' What would you do? Would you just leave?...The Asháninkas' reason to be is having land. But if the dam floods the valley, where I am going to go? It would be like disappearing."

For weeks, Buendía visited Asháninka communities to inform people about the impact of Pakitzapango. She also travelled by bus from Satipo to Lima to interview officials from the Ministry of Energy and Mining. For two years, she tried. The response was always the same: That they were sorry, that they could not do anything, that the project was in the country's best interest.

So, she started a campaign to expose the risks to the Asháninka, travelling to Washington DC in 2010 to bring a lawsuit against the Peruvian government at the Inter-American Commission on Human Rights. She visited environmental ministers and bankers and investors who financed hydroelectric projects in a dozen countries. She met with executives from the construction company and Brazil's ministries of energy and foreign relations. She warned them what would happen if they built the dam on Asháninka land. "But if despite everything they don't listen to us, blood will be shed," she told them. "If our government does not respect us then we will make them respect us."

At the end of 2010, the Commission on Human Rights asked the Peruvian government to guarantee the protection of Asháninka land. They couldn't, and it forced them to stop the project. A year later, the dam company backed out of the project, saying they would respect the Indigenous people's decision.

Ruth Buendía and CARE had been able to paralyze the development without marching, burning tires or blocking roads.

For her efforts, Buendía won the Goldman Prize in 2014, considered the most important environmental award in the world.

So, all is well now? Hardly. One current threat is from Pluspetrol, the main producer of gas and oil in Peru. In 2005, the Peruvian government gave them a concession in the Amazon territory for more than a million hectares where natural gas and light crude oil are abundant. The problem is that the entire Ene River valley—where more than 20,000 Asháninkas live—is inside this area. In the northern part of this sector, the sounds of helicopters are common and workers cut roads to set off explosives. In the southern part, however, the oil company still has not done anything—the Asháninkas do not let them. "The communities are well informed. They know their rights. They can't cheat them anymore."

However, elsewhere in Peru, Pluspetrol Norte has been given 72 fines exceeding $47 million between 2011 and 2021 for its oil spills, which doesn't begin to cover the cost of repair for the affected areas.

Today, Buendía continues her work for CARE and also takes on roles outside of the organization, including a position as secretary of the Inter-Ethnic Association for the Development of the Peruvian Amazon, who advocate for inclusive education in Indigenous territories.

No matter what challenges she faces, Buendía always comes back to finding strength in her roots: "On my back, I carry my culture, my territory, my family, and my ancestors that came before me, which I need to defend."

The Asháninkas' reason to be is having land. But if the dam floods the valley, where I am going to go? It would be like disappearing."

Photos courtesy of Goldman Environmental Prize

RACHEL CARSON

Rachel Carson ~ Maryland, USA

"Knowing what I do, there would be no future peace for me if I kept silent," Rachel Carson wrote in a letter to her closest friend Dorothy Freeman, ninety days before the release of her 1962 book *Silent Spring*. She added a quote from an old poem, "To sin by silence, when we should protest, makes cowards out of men."

Though she had earned a Master's Degree in zoology at Johns Hopkins University in 1932, Carson was an outsider to the scientific establishment. She didn't have a Ph.D, she didn't write for scientists but for the general public as editor-in-chief for the U.S. Fish and Wildlife Service, and perhaps worst of all in the 1950s, she was a woman.

"It is one of the ironies of our time that, while concentrating on the defense of our country against enemies from without, we should be so heedless of those who would destroy it from within."

Soon after Dwight Eisenhower took office in 1952, the Republican administration placed a nonscientist as head of the USFWS who immediately politicized the office. Carson courageously responded to the ensuing political exploitation in a 1953 letter to the editor of the Washington Post:

"For many years public-spirited citizens throughout the country have been working for the conservation of the natural resources, realizing their vital importance to the Nation. Apparently their hard-won progress is to be wiped out, as a politically-minded Administration returns us to the dark ages of unrestrained exploitation and destruction...It is one of the ironies of our time that, while concentrating on the defense of our country against enemies from without, we should be so heedless of those who would destroy it from within."

Carson wasn't new to the public. She published her first book, *Under the Sea Wind*, in 1941, then *The Sea Around Us* in 1951, and later would publish *The Edge of the Sea* in 1955, all of which made Rachel Carson the foremost science writer in America. She won the

National Book Award for nonfiction, was elected to the American Academy of Arts and Letters, and in her 1952 acceptance speech for the John Burroughs Medal, she sermonized: "It seems reasonable to believe—and I do believe—that the more clearly we can focus our attention on the wonders and realities of the universe about us the less taste we shall have for the destruction of our race. Wonder and humility are wholesome emotions, and they do not exist side by side with a lust for destruction."

She had a nearly impossible uphill battle against post-World War II science and technology that was given free rein, including the use of toxic chemicals like DDT that were lauded as miracles of science. Science was considered both divinely inspired and male, and the multimillion dollar chemical industry that initially tried to dismiss her soon turned on her in a fury. Why? Carson insisted that what science conceived and technology made possible must first be judged for its safety and benefit to the "whole stream of life." Carson advocated for moral responsibility, challenging the wisdom and hubris of applying toxic chemicals onto land and water before knowing the long-term consequences of their use.

In January of 1958, Carson received a letter from Olga Owens

Huckins, describing how the aerial spraying of DDT had devastated a local wildlife sanctuary and resulted in the ghastly deaths of birds, "claws clutched to their breasts and bills agape in agony." She had been collecting a dossier of evidence on the toxicity of various chemicals and their deadly impacts on wildlife when Huckins's letter jolted her into developing her findings into a book, a decision that resulted in the publication of *Silent Spring* in 1962.

In the book, Carson describes how chlorinated hydrocarbons and organic phosphorus insecticides alter the cellular processes of plants, animals, and thus humans—a complicated process. But she knew how to bring science down to earth, writing in a language that everyone could understand, and asking questions that everyone had a right to ask; questions like, "Can anyone believe it is possible to lay down such a barrage of poisons on the surface of the earth without making it unfit for all life?"

She was one of the first to declare what is so obvious today but which is still so often disregarded, that human beings are simply one of nature's parts, and the survival of one part depends upon the health of all.

The scientific and chemical establishment responded with a barrage of condemnation and insults. She was an "hysterical woman," they said, a "bird and bunny lover," a "romantic spinster" out of control who had overstepped her bounds both scientifically and culturally.

Former Secretary of Agriculture Ezra Taft Benson wrote privately to former President Dwight Eisenhower that Carson was "probably a communist" and asked: "Why a spinster with no children was so concerned about genetics?"

Carson was linked to "food faddists" or, as William Darby of the Vanderbilt University School of Medicine characterized them, "the organic gardeners, the anti-fluoride leaguers, the worshippers of 'natural foods.'"

An agricultural expert told a reporter at a government hearing on insecticides, "You're never going to satisfy organic farmers or emotional women in garden clubs."

A book reviewer in *Time* magazine criticized her "emotion-fanning words" and characterized her argument as "unfair, one-sided, and hysterically overemphatic." He traced her "emotional and inaccurate outburst" to her "mystical attachment to the balance of nature."

And one letter to the editor of the *New Yorker* said perhaps what a lot of men thought at the time: "Miss Rachel Carson's reference to the selfishness of insecticide manufacturers probably reflects her Communist sympathies, like a lot of our writers these days. We can live without birds and animals, but, as the current market slump shows, we cannot live without business. As for insects, isn't it just like a woman to be scared to death of a few little bugs! As long as we have the H-bomb everything will be O.K."

In the midst of writing the book, Carson was diagnosed with cancer in 1960, and so was being attacked both from without and within. She would die in the spring of 1964 at the age of fifty-six, and was posthumously awarded the Presidential Medal of Freedom in 1981.

She never lived to witness the sea change of policy and public awareness that her book put into motion, a course of events that resulted in the 1972 ban of the domestic production of DDT and the grass-roots movements that brought about Federal policies like the establishment of the EPA and the Clean Water Act.

Perhaps most importantly, Carson remains an example of what one committed individual can do to protect the rights of all life, and how while one's work may be furiously attacked, it can shift the future. She noted early on that when the public protested against toxins, it was "fed little tranquillizing pills of half-truth" by a morally-challenged government that refused to acknowledge evidence of damage.

Carson, on the other hand, fed us the whole truth.

Hawk watching: Photo by Shirley A. Briggs

By permission of Rachel Carson Council, Inc.

*"Knowing what I do, there would be no future
peace for me if I kept silent."*

ACARE/AWIS— AFRICAN GREAT LAKES

Catherine Ajuna Fridolin, Elizabeth Wambui Wanderi, Margret Sindat ~ Africa

Catherine Ajuna Fridolin is an aquatic and fisheries scientist currently pursuing a Master of Science in Fisheries and Aquaculture at the University of Dar Es Salaam in Tanzania. She has worked on Lake Victoria where her biggest aspirations are to see the amplification of women's voices in water-related fields and to see more women involved in the field.

"As a woman, people close to me didn't believe me when I told them I wanted to become an aquatic scientist. They thought I was too ambitious, especially for a field that has been largely dominated by men for a long time now. But I did actually break the barriers by doing what I was told I wouldn't do, and I intend to continue doing big things in the field. I look forward to future collaborations and training that will help me to reach my goals and prove that what a man can do, a woman can do also, even better."

"I love field work, mainly working with communities by teaching them best practices on how to sustainably manage natural resources."

Elizabeth Wambui Wanderi works in the Lake Turkana Region as a fisheries officer for the Kenya Fisheries Service, managing, developing and conserving the fisheries resources of Lake Turkana. She is also researching how to maximize production in Nile tilapia (*Oreochromis niloticus*) cage farming in Lake Victoria while pursuing her Master of Science degree in Aquaculture at Kisii University, Kenya. Her research interests include fisheries management, aquaculture, and food security.

"My inspiration is drawn from the challenges of water scarcity in my region. Being born in northern Kenya, a semi-arid region with no streams or rivers nearby, we depended on underground salt water, rainwater or tapped dammed water, which was scarce. We had to travel long distances during dry seasons when the dam water was no longer sufficient for everyone to fetch water for domestic use...[Now] I love working with communities living around, and utilizing, aquatic ecosystems, and sensitizing them on how to protect and conserve resources... What matters the most is seeing the community around our freshwater ecosystems benefiting from the resources to improve their living standards, and at the same time, conserving it for future generations."

Margret Sindat is currently pursuing her Master's Degree in Aquaculture at Lilongwe University of Agriculture and Natural Resources in Malawi. She is researching newer technologies in fish processing. Sindat is also doing an internship under Sustainable Fisheries and Aquaculture where she prepares and implements project activities to increase the recovery of fish stocks through watershed management. She hopes to reduce poverty through increasing income from fisheries, increasing healthy fish consumption, and strengthening nutritional security.

"I love field work, mainly working with communities by teaching them best practices on how to sustainably manage natural resources...Lake Malawi has more than 1,000 fish species. Currently, the lake is threatened by climate change, overuse of resources and pollution among others.

"What matters most about my work is delivering quality results in a timely manner. I love analyzing water quality parameters from the lake and other drinking water sources, because I believe that water is life."

ACARE/AWIS—
AFRICAN GREAT LAKES

Donnata Alupot, Marie Claire Dusabe,
Diane Umutoni ~ Africa

As a professional meteorologist on Lake Victoria, **Donnata Alupot** works as the lead coordinator in developing the project "Strengthening Meteorological Services to Increase Resilience in Uganda." Here she analyses weather systems, monitors severe weather events, and issues warnings and advisories about severe weather events. Her focus is on increasing the resilience of communities around Lake Victoria through using impact-based forecasting and warning services.

"I love being a part of solving a problem, I love being a part of a solution that contributes positively to people's lives. and I'm inspired by what I can contribute to saving people's lives on the Lakes."

"I want us to be aware of the state of water quality in our region, so that we can conserve it, as well as the organisms that live in it."

Marie Claire Dusabe is currently doing her PhD in Animal Ecology and Systematics in Giessen, Germany. Her goal is to develop a biotic index for the lakes of the East African Rift Valley using macroinvertebrates. She has studied the entire Congo Basin on the Rwandan side, where she worked on 59 Congo Basin rivers to assess their water quality based on macroinvertebrate diversity. She was named a Wildlife Warrior 2019, a Conservation Hero 2019 and a National Geographic Explorer 2019.

"I do what I do only because water is so precious... It is important to me that everyone has the right to clean and safe water and that our native aquatic organisms are preserved.

"I grew up in Rubavu district of western Rwanda near Lake Kivu and have always been aware of water issues—particularly the severe water pollution in my neighborhood...I want us to be aware of the state of water quality in our region, so that we can conserve it, as well as the organisms that live in it."

Diane Umutoni currently works as a Conservation and Research Assistant at Akagera National Park in Rwanda, carrying out fisheries monitoring and management in the park. Akagera National Park is Central Africa's largest protected wetland. Umutoni holds a Master's degree in Hydrobiology from China and a Bachelor's degree in Wildlife and Aquatic Resources Management from Rwanda. All of her work derives from her belief that "water is life."

ACARE/AWIS—
AFRICAN GREAT LAKES

*Grite Nelson Mwaijengo, Gladys Chigamba,
Esther Kagoya ~ Africa*

Freshwater ecologist **Grite Nelson Mwaijengo**
holds a PhD in biology, and is currently working as a
lecturer and researcher at the Nelson Mandela African
Institution of Science and Technology in Arusha,
Tanzania. Mwaijengo's main research interests span the
development and use of GIS-remote sensing and eco-
hydrological tools in the assessment and monitoring
of freshwater ecosystems. Specifically, Mwaijengo is
interested in developing and using biological indices to
improve the health of the freshwater ecosystems. She
is keenly interested in influencing policy and decision-
making processes on sustainable management of the
freshwater ecosystems in Tanzania and the East African
Great Lakes.

"The value we got from the water was the inspiration to take care of it."

Academically trained as a fisheries scientist at Lilongwe
University of Agriculture and Natural Resources,
Gladys Chigamba in Malawi is a researcher in the field
of aquaculture and fisheries management. Recently
she carried out research in estimating the economic
valuation of river ecosystems in Malawi. Her study
revealed the high value that riverine ecosystems have on
human livelihoods. She hopes to expand her research
to cover a wider number of rivers to determine their
specific values.

"I was born in Zimbabwe from a Malawian father
and Zimbabwean mother. We migrated from Zimbabwe
to Malawi when I was really young. Malawi is nicknamed
'warm heart of Africa'. Most importantly, it is known for
its extraordinary freshwater lake, Lake Malawi. I grew up
hearing the statement; 'water is life'. Our village was close
to the water site, and we used to get most
of our resources from this water site:
food, recreation, bathing, timber etc.

"There are many people who
inspired me in water issues, but my
uncle was the greatest of all. For years I
watched him taking care of water sources
as a fisherman. He would take me along
for fishing, though society restricts
females from the activity. The value we
got from the water was the inspiration to
take care of it."

Ester Kagoya is a socio-economist
who worked as a research assistant
on assessment of fish stocks in Lake
Victoria.

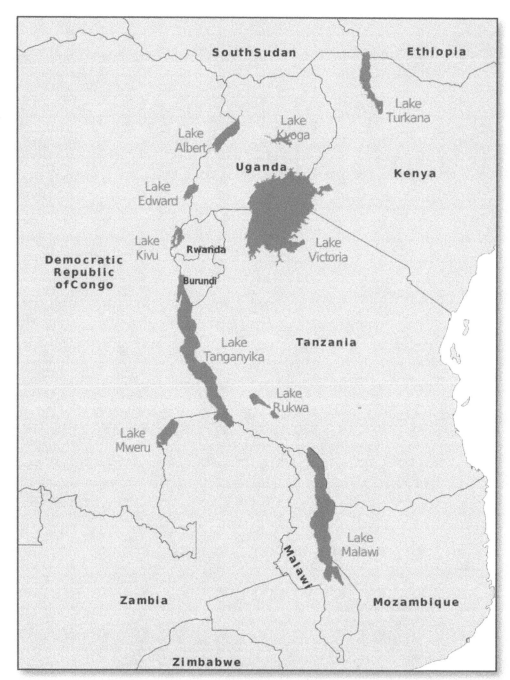

THE AFRICAN GREAT LAKES

*"I love field work, mainly working with communities
by teaching them best practices on how to sustainably
manage natural resources...Lake Malawi has more
than 1,000 fish species. Currently, the lake is threatened
by climate change, overuse of resources and pollution
among others."* - Margret Sindat

Esther Kagoya, Diane Umutoni, Marie Claire Dusabe, Catherine Ajuna Fridolin, Grite Nelson Mwaijengo, Margret Sindat, Elizabeth Wambui Wanderi, Gladys Chigamba, Donnata Alupot

GREAT LAKES/ACARE/AWIS

The African Great Lakes

The African Great Lakes constitute about 25% of the Earth's unfrozen fresh water, more than either North America's Great Lakes or Lake Baikal in Russia. The nine lakes include Lake Victoria, the second-largest fresh water lake in the world by area; Lake Tanganyika, the world's second-largest freshwater lake by volume and depth; Lake Turkana, the world's largest permanent desert and alkaline lake; and Lake Malawi, the world's eighth-largest freshwater lake by area. The lakes harbor the most productive freshwater fisheries in the world, and contain over 10% of all species of freshwater fish in the world. They form the headwaters to the three great rivers of Africa: The Nile, the Congo, and the Zambezi, all of which are global treasures of aquatic diversity.

Over 107 million people live around these lakes, many of which are threatened by over-exploitation, urban and industrial pollution, agricultural runoff, and looming worries over climate change. And each lake varies in its biophysical characteristics, ecological and economic concerns, governance, and potential sustainable development.

African Center for Aquatic Research and Education (ACARE)

ACARE provides an innovative learning experience for young freshwater experts in the African Great Lakes riparian countries of Uganda, Kenya, Tanzania, Ethiopia, Rwanda, Burundi, DR Congo, Zambia, Malawi, and Mozambique. It helps talented African scientists and aquatic resource managers develop hands-on skills and engage in professional networks that will better allow them to remain in their fields within the region. The entire focus of ACARE is to ensure that the ecological structure of the African Great Lakes is preserved and enhanced for local communities.

ACARE's vision is to help bring into existence a world where millions of Africans can depend on healthy African Great Lakes for food, clean water, and reliable employment, supporting a climate of justice, equity, democracy, and peace.

African Women in Science (AWIS)

ACARE is also working to enhance the participation of women in solving critical freshwater issues, knowing that limited representation of women in science reduces the perspective, knowledge, and efforts of half of the population. Because women have been disenfranchised from work in the sciences, ACARE seeks to change this through training, education, and mentoring in its African Women in Science program. AWIS' mission is to support and guide African women scientists to catalyze positive change on the African Great Lakes and their tributaries.

The annual 10-month-long program builds capacity for African women in science through professional development. It also advances science on the African Great Lakes and their tributaries by adding more women scientists' wisdom and research to the scientific community.

CAROL WARDEN
AND EMILY STANLEY

Carol Warden ~ Wisconsin, USA

For years, **Carol Warden** met with lake groups that were seeing marked changes in their lakes due to invasive species or changes in water quality. A scientist educator at the University of Wisconsin-Trout Lake Limnology Station in northern Wisconsin, she worked hands-on studying individual

Photo courtesy of Carol Warden

lakes and their aquatic plants, insects and fish, as well as with people, always striving to find common goals for how people can be the best stewards of "their" lakes.

Trout Lake Station is located in Vilas County, a globally important area for freshwater lakes, with one of the highest densities of lakes in the world. Some two million people visit the area every year to enjoy this fresh water, so as with all beautiful places, one of the questions for researchers is how to help the public become ecologically literate so they don't love a place to death.

In the past, Warden divided her time between collecting and analyzing aquatic plant data throughout a nine-county region, educating the public on invasive species, and working with lake groups to secure funding for lake protection and management projects. Most recently, Warden has been collecting and analyzing data for the North Temperate Lakes Long-Term Ecological Research (LTER) program, a project in continuous operation on area lakes since 1981. This has been foundational in capturing changes and nuances in these lakes that are valued so dearly. The continuity provides perspective that can't be found with just one short visit.

Warden was raised on a small lake in northern Wisconsin where she learned to swim, fish, paddle, and observe lake life. That upbringing and a subsequent Master of Science degree in Water Resources

Management fed her soul. She writes, "Water is Life. I'm passionate about this truth. From our most basic needs to our most treasured memories, water is front and center. I cannot overstate how blessed we are in Northern Wisconsin to be so water rich; and not only in terms of abundance of water but the quality of our water also. Protecting that blessing for generations to come is crucial."

She is driven to help people become aware that what we do in and around water matters. The key, she says, is to "tread lightly, be respectful, educate ourselves on how we move things around and how our actions have an impact."

Carol Warden isn't famous (at least not yet). She's one of thousands of scientist educators who aren't household names, but who matter deeply to their local communities. She still occasionally tromps around in shallow waters with school children to find aquatic insects, identify them, and teach their value in the larger community of life. She gets people of all ages into the water, out in the "weeds," to demonstrate that the plants aren't weeds, but essential members of the life of a lake, without which we wouldn't have fish and herons and loons and otters.

Warden does her work out of love for fresh waters, for the myriad lifeforms they support, and for the people who live on them and need to love them, too, in order to do the work of protecting them.

Photo courtesy of Emily Stanley

Emily Stanley ~ Wisconsin, USA

Emily Stanley, a nationally known, award-winning professor and researcher at the Center for Limnology at the University of Wisconsin-Madison, has been taking on some very big questions. Among other studies, Stanley is part of a group seeking to understand and predict global nutrient patterns of nitrogen, phosphorus, and carbon for ALL continental U.S. lakes. First, she's helping to build a large, integrated database that includes measures of *in situ* nutrients and other ecological metrics collected from over 130,000 lakes. Then, she and her colleagues intend to try to answer a series of enormous ecological questions on this continental scale.

Stanley has consistently pushed scientists to look beyond traditional physical and disciplinary boundaries of freshwater research. Her early research explored the linkages between stream nutrient dynamics, sediment transport, large-scale geomorphic changes and dam removal—research that provided critical data to natural resource managers.

More recently, Stanley has been playing a leading role in improving the understanding of methane production in flowing waters and its potential to contribute to global carbon cycles. This, too, has involved building a database to take on questions about the role of world rivers in releasing methane to the atmosphere.

Stanley is also known for her research on streams where she is currently trying to "measure the pulse of streams" in a study she calls "The Stream Pulse Project."

Another of her research projects has been given the acronym FLAMe, for "Fast Limnology Automated Measurements." Her graduate students built a contraption that consists of a water pump, a series of pipes and tubes, and $100,000-worth of sensors. As their boat moves across the surface of the Mississippi River, a continuous stream of water is sucked into the FLAMe and passed over sensors which record everything from turbidity to temperature to nitrate levels, before the water is discharged back into the river.

"At the heart of the FLAMe are these automated sensors that are commercially available and widely used by limnologists everywhere," says Stanley. "But what [researchers] usually do is park them on a buoy or put them in a particular place in a stream and they get really good data at that site over time. With the FLAMe, instead of parking these devices in one place, we bring the water

to the devices and take the devices everywhere...We don't have that spatial understanding of our ecosystem in the same way that a terrestrial ecologist does. The FLAMe gives us a whole new way of seeing lakes and rivers that we just haven't had before."

Stanley's influence in freshwater research extends far beyond her own research and lab in Madison. As Principal Investigator at the North Temperate Lakes Long-Term Ecological Research (NTL-LTER) site, she provides strong leadership to a large team of NTL-LTER researchers, formulating research questions and field studies in both northern Wisconsin's Vilas County and Dane County in southern Wisconsin.

She co-edited the 2016 book *Stream Ecosystems in a Changing Environment*. And in 2018, she was the recipient of the G. Evelyn Hutchinson Award from the Association for the Sciences of Limnology and Oceanography, which honors a limnologist or oceanographer who has made considerable contributions to knowledge, and whose future work promises a continued legacy of scientific excellence. That same year she was named a Fellow by the Ecological Society of American for "the quality and importance of her contributions to ecology, for her ability to identify and lead new ecological frontiers, and for making connections across boundaries that continue to push our field forward." And that same year the Society for Freshwater Sciences also named her a Fellow.

Perhaps just as importantly, she is a well-loved professor known for her sense of humor as well as her scholarly research.

"We can leave a legacy, or we can leave a scar." - Carol Warden

"We're monkeying with the very chemical foundation of these ecosystems. But right now we don't know enough yet to know where we're going. To me, scientifically that's really interesting, and as a human, a little bit frightening." - Emily Stanley

IKAL ANGELEI

Ikal Angelei ~ Kenya

Lake Turkana is the largest desert lake in the world. A UNESCO World Heritage Site, it is located in the Kenyan Rift Valley in northern Kenya, with its far northern end crossing into Ethiopia. An archeological site where some of the oldest human fossils have been found, the Lake Turkana Basin is home to large populations of crocodiles, hippos, snakes, and fish, but also serves as a lifeline to hundreds of thousands of indigenous farmers, herders, and fisherpeople who live around it.

In 2006, Ethiopia began construction of the Gibe 3 Dam along the Omo River, the upstream source of 90 percent of Lake Turkana's water. When completed, the dam was to be the largest hydroelectric plant in Africa, the fourth largest in the world.

> *"Whatever I am fighting for here in Kenya, links to the voices in Chad, links to the voices in Mexico, links to the voices of the Sami—because the geographies may be different, but the issues are the same."*

Why build such a giant dam? By 2025, Ethiopia envisions being a fully decarbonized economy providing 100% of its electricity needs to not only cover internal demand, but also to export, an admirable goal in this era of climate change.

However, green economic development projects can have environmental costs as well as exacerbate social injustices. The issue: The dam was projected to cause the lake's water level to drop by as much as 23 to 33 feet within the first five years, depleting fish stocks and depriving communities of a critical source of potable water in this desert environment.

When Ikal Angelei heard about the construction of the massive dam, she became outraged at the fact that plans were moving forward without any consultation with local communities. In response, she founded the group Friends of Lake Turkana (FoLT) in 2008, following in the footsteps of her father, a distinguished member

Photos courtesy of Goldman Environmental Prize

of the Kenyan Parliament who had opposed the construction of the 502-foot-tall Turkwell Dam two decades earlier.

Angelei brought together Lake Turkana's divided and marginalized indigenous communities, all of whom had not heard about the dam, to fight against the potential environmental and social costs of the Gibe 3 Dam. She took their voices to local members of parliament and Kenya's Ministries of Environment, Energy, Water and Irrigation and Fisheries, urging them to rethink the dam given its implications.

In angry response, Ethiopian Prime Minister Meles Zenawi vowed to complete the dam in 2010 "at any cost," saying about critics of the dam: "They don't want to see a developed Africa; they want us to remain undeveloped and backward to serve their tourists as a museum."

Nevertheless, due in part to Angelei's advocacy, in August 2011, the Kenyan Parliament demanded an independent environmental assessment from Ethiopia. UNESCO's World Heritage Committee also passed a resolution to halt dam construction until further investigations were made. Additionally, Angelei successfully helped convinced major banks, including the World Bank, the European Investment Bank, and the African Development Bank, to withdraw their financing of the Gibe 3 Dam due to the adverse social and environmental impacts, leaving the Chinese Export Import Bank as the major investor.

For these efforts, Angelei was awarded the prestigious Goldman Environmental Prize in 2012.

But the fight was nowhere near over. In September 2012, while China continued to fund the dam, the China Export Import Bank signed a memorandum of understanding with the Ethiopia Sugar Corporation for the construction of sugar factories in the Lower Omo Valley, which would need irrigation water from the GIBE 3 to produce sugar cane.

Soon after, FoLT filed a court case challenging Kenya's move to buy electricity from Ethiopia, which would deprive community members living within the Lake Basin of their constitutional rights to life and dignity.

Unfortunately, the court could not prohibit the government of Kenya from entering into further agreements with the Ethiopian Government to purchase 500MW from Gibe 3. However, the court did declare that the community's right to information was violated when information on the power purchase and other impacts of Gibe 3 were withheld, affirming that the government of Kenya must disclose all relevant information to the communities involved.

 The Gibe 3 Dam was ultimately completed in 2016, doubling Ethiopian hydroelectric hydropower capacity, and water levels in Lake Turkana have dropped by approximately 1.5 meters (5 feet) so far. With Ethiopia's plan for two additional upstream dams, Gibe 4 and Gibe 5, further water reduction is expected, with dire effects predicted to the Lake's ecosystem.

Angelei says, "While the Ethiopian government holds that the dams will not adversely affect the communities, we continue to push for independent Environmental and Social Impact Assessments to be done that examine the cumulative impacts...You cannot alter nature; you cannot fight nature...Lake Turkana doesn't have an outlet; it is a closed lake. So, it depends on that balance of inflow versus evaporation.

If you reduce that inflow, the level of evaporation increases. Once you have altered the balance of the lake, you have damaged the ecosystem completely.

"But for us, it has always been: At what expense? And what alternatives do we have? I think it is a human rights abuse and an environmental abuse. You cannot say 'development' is telling people that your way of life doesn't work anymore. People have to develop in the way they see fit. If I don't want to drive, it doesn't mean I'm not developed. It means I am living my life in the way I see fit, as long as I am able to achieve my spiritual and basic needs.

"So, our big goal is to push for comprehensive, independent environmental and social impact assessments of the entire basin, which would allow us to understand what opportunities we have; what challenges we have; how fragile this ecosystem is; and what sort of development can be done there. And it would allow the communities to be part of this discussion."

By 2020, four years after the completion of the Gibe 3 dam, various predicted negative outcomes had become a reality. Gibe 3 dam altered the magnitude and seasonality of the Omo River flood pulse tremendously, since 90% of the lake's freshwater inflow originates from the river. The dam ended the natural annual flooding over the banks of the Omo River, which replenished the thin soil with enough nutrients to sprout grass for cattle and allowed the cultivation of crops like corn and sorghum. Local ecosystems largely depend on this flood pulse. The pulse sustains a biodiverse delta, and produces lake level oscillations that are vital to nutrient circulation, fish spawning, and the regeneration of lakeshore grazing areas for livestock, a crucial protein source for the 300,000 people inhabiting the poorest region in Kenya.

An artificial regulated flow through the dam was intended to mimic this natural flood pulse, but the dam traps sediment. So, even with regulated flow, there are still impacts on wildlife and farming because of the reduced nutrients from this sediment.

In addition, Gibe 3 dam's river regulation enabled the Ethiopian Government to develop large-scale irrigation plantations. Already, 100,000 hectares (240,000 acres) within the Omo Basin have been transformed into water-intensive sugar plantations, and downstream, 50,000 hectares (70,000 acres) have been allocated to a foreign cotton plantation company. A landscape-scale transformation is occurring in which commodities, rather than staple foods for local consumption, are becoming the main output of the region.

As the lake level falls, the water's salinity and temperature increase. These changes threaten the habitat, breeding grounds, and food sources for fish stocks and grazing areas along the lake's shoreline. Increased salinity and runoff containing pollutants from pesticides and fertilizers will also increase health risks of the lake water used for human consumption.

To further complicate the issue, Ethiopia's water resources are highly sensitive to climate change. Climate change will impact the availability and seasonality of fresh water because of expected climate extremes, such as heat waves, meteorological and hydrological droughts, and changes in rainfall patterns.

So, the battle continues. Angelei says, "We remain persistent in our fight for the lake, pushing for the stop of additional destructive projects along the Basin, demanding the monitoring of the filling of the dams, and following up on international efforts such as engaging UNESCO to maintain the endangered status of Lake Turkana until both countries show implementable and effective mitigation measures...Our resolve is strong and our fight unrelenting."

Angelei recognizes that her local efforts for indigenous voices to be heard and valued is really a much broader battle. "Whether it's the Asian or African continent or the Global South, it's finding ways and means to connect these voices, and make them the center of conversations—not just when and if needed. Also, it's important that these voices are not siloed, and that we really find ways to connect these voices. So, whatever I am fighting for here in Kenya, links to the voices in Chad, links to the voices in Mexico, links to the voices of the Sami—because the geographies may be different, but the issues are the same."

(Note: Besides other dams on the Omo river, Ethiopia is now building the largest hydropower plant of Africa, the GERD (Grand Ethiopian Renaissance Dam), on the Blue Nile river, leading to tensions between Ethiopia and Egypt.

Hydropower is the dominant renewable electricity source worldwide. Almost 500 dams are planned worldwide in regions influenced by climate change.)

Photos courtesy of Goldman Environmental Prize

SHARON DAY

Sharon Day ~ Minnesota, USA

"We are not a protest. We are a prayer for the water ...As Indigenous people, we believe water has a spirit. It's that spirit we're speaking to every time we walk." So speaks Sharon Day, a Water Walker, a member of the Bois Forte Band of Ojibwe in Minnesota, and the founder of *Nibi* ("Water") Walk, an organization that coordinates Indigenous-led water walks in the United States to promote people's spiritual and physical relationship with water.

In 2003, when Grandmother Josephine Mandamin walked around Lake Superior, Day walked with her for two days on the eastern shore near Lake Superior Provincial Park in Ontario. Since then, she has led 20 water walks to call attention to pollution in rivers, lakes and oceans, and to "heal the water" because in doing so, "we heal all life." She has walked major rivers like the Missouri in 2017, starting from its headwaters in Montana, and 54 days later, reaching its confluence with Mississippi. And she's walked smaller rivers like the Cuyahoga in Ohio on the 50th anniversary of it famously catching fire, travelling for three days in 2019 for nearly 100 miles from its headwaters to its union with Lake Erie in Cleveland.

"When we drink water, we are drinking the same water our grandparents and our ancestors drank since the beginning of time. We are the ancestors, and we are the ancestors yet to come. Be loving, be kind and I will try to do the same, too. Migwetch."

Every walk is an extended ceremony and has the same spirit and goal. She says, "We hope that as we walk, people become more connected to these waterways and have this realization that water is life...Hopefully people will have gained enough knowledge and rekindle that love for the water."

In 2013, Day, along with others who joined her along the way, carried a pail of water from the headwaters of the Mississippi River in Itaska, Minnesota, to Fort Jackson, Louisiana, south of New Orleans. There, after 65 days of walking, they poured the clean water into the river, and she noted, "We wanted to give the river a taste of herself—the way she began—and tell her: 'This is how we wish you will be again.'"

Photo courtesy of Sharon Day

At the moment she poured the water back into the Mississippi River, "There was a wave that came over our feet. The last wave reached our knees. It was almost as if we were being kissed by the river," she said, reinforcing her belief that there is a deep personal connection between people and water.

"It's not just that we love the river," she added, "but that the river loves us."

Walking these great distances while praying and singing all along the way, she inspires people to come into a deeper understanding of their relationship to water. The hope is that the walks are transformational: "In walking and having people join me...I realized there's another way to change the world. And it's by having people reconnect with the water."

Day has walked the Ohio River, the St. Louis River, the Cuyahoga River, the James River, the Chippewa River, the Minnesota River, Minnehaha Creek, the Kettle River, the Potomac River, the Missouri River, the Wisconsin River, Phalen Creek, the Chicago River, the Cannon River, the Red River, Lake Pokegema, the Mississippi River, and the Salt River.

She is the Executive Director of the Indigenous Peoples Task Force, based in Minneapolis, Minnesota, and is also a grandmother, artist, musician, and writer. In 2021, she had planned with others to again walk the length of the Mississippi River, this time bringing the water from the dead zone in the Gulf of Mexico near Fort Jackson, Louisiana, to the headwaters in Itasca, Minnesota, for healing. But COVID-19 derailed the walk, and the walk is now rescheduled for 2023.

In August 2023, on the twenty year anniversary of Grandmother Josphine Mandamin's first Nibi Walk around Lake Superior, Day will retrace her steps. This 33 day walk will begin around July 31 in the Duluth area and travel clockwise around the lake. All people are invited to join for any length of time at any place along the journey.

"We do this to honor the water, to speak to the water and to let her know that there are still people who love and care for the water."

Photo courtesy of Sharon Day

If we can we slow down
Walk quietly
Speak silently to the spirit of the water
If we can participate in ceremony daily
It becomes part of our being
Our conscious and subconscious
If we can disconnect from the harsh news of the day
Focus on the mist in the air at daybreak
Our voices rise together
To greet the sun
As we hold our asemaa
And sing to the four directions
ni mama Aki and all that there is
If we can slow down or withdraw slightly from our interactions with the world around us
We hasten our brain functionality, our capacity to feel and care for others
Including the flowers, the butterflies, the birds, and our spiritual growth accelerates
If our spiritual growth is a communal process
Our collective physical, emotional and spiritual growth
Is accelerated as we walk up and down the hills and byways along the river
carrying the water or the staff
and especially if our physical self is taxed in this process.
If the hills are larger, our tendency is to move faster and as we approach the confluence,
we run, run, run.
Together
We grow, we grow, we grow!

Sharon Day, September 14, 2018

"I have been thinking in the depths of my own despair, how did the people, my great grandparents, your great-great grandparents, move forward out of despair they must have felt in the late 1800's and early 1900's? A time when our people had been removed to reservations. Moved to land that might have been unfamiliar to them, land that was not large enough to sustain all the people especially if they were nations that hunted and gathered? Even agrarian nations did not have enough land to grow the foods to feed the families. They were victims of massacres, biological warfare, and starvation. They killed the buffalo herds, cut down the trees...there must have been great despair and a deep, deep depression. So how did they move forward?"

"Perhaps they lived their lives. They went foraging in the springtime, tapped the maple trees, they harvested wild rice in the fall and set their snares for the wabooze in the winter. They cut wood to keep themselves warm. They used the rabbit fur for mittens and the deer hide for leggings and moccasins. When they picked that odemin in the spring, and they tasted that red berry, shaped like a heart, they knew they were going to be okay. I like to think I am here today, because my great-great-grandparents loved each other, and they loved me before I was born. It is that love that moves us forward."

Photo courtesy of Sharon Day

KATHLEEN CARPENTER

Kathleen Carpenter ~ Wales

"Fathers" of various scientific disciplines are common, but "Mothers"? Rare indeed.

Perhaps one of the first to break that glass ceiling was Kathleen Carpenter, later called "The Mother of Freshwater Ecology" thanks to her pioneering early-20th century limnology work in Wales.

Born in 1891, Carpenter researched the impact of acid mine waters on the ecology of Welsh rivers, some of which were nearly devoid of life. She proved that suffocation due to the development of a film on the gills was the cause of death for coldwater fish like salmon and trout in rivers polluted by metallic mine wastes.

Silver, lead and zinc had been mined in Wales since Roman times, and some historical evidence linked mine wastewater to ecological damage. As early as 1861, one report declared "a total extinction of animal life" in the rivers Rheidol and Ystwyth.

"It [inland waters] is a world of infinite beauty, infinite variety, infinite charm."

RIVER YSTWYTH

But it wasn't until nearly 60 years later in 1919 that Carpenter's survey of the River Ystwyth showed that mining activity in the area was the direct cause of the river's fauna being reduced to nine species, mostly insects.

The river fauna weren't the only ones dying. Miners at the Cwm Ystwyth mine on the River Ystwyth died on

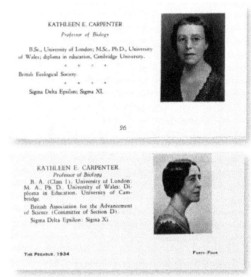

Photos courtesy of Aberystwyth University

average at age 32, largely because of acute lead poisoning.

Carpenter studied other rivers as well, including the River Rheidol, where she found a very scant algal and bryophyte flora and fauna limited to 14 species, all aquatic invertebrates.

She worked initially at a time when cars were just becoming available, and women were altering their conservative clothing so they could carry out fieldwork. The first women to undertake aquatic field biology did so encumbered with long sleeves, hats and long skirts. However, the First World War helped to partially change social norms in Britain, and women soon adopted trousers and more practical clothes.

Carpenter attended and worked at universities in Europe and the US which pioneered the education of women. She entered University College Wales (Aberystwyth) in 1907, and was awarded a B.Sc. in 1910 and, subsequently earned a M.Sc. and PhD at Aberystwyth.

Her meticulous sampling protocol included collecting organisms from the sediments, from within the water column, from the vegetation, and from the water surface. This research led her to produce comprehensive species lists of river and stream organisms, as well as one of the first representations of freshwater food webs in Britain.

Carpenter's work showed the ecological resilience of river ecosystems. If allowed time, they could largely restore themselves. The rivers she studied exhibited a classic pattern of biological recolonization following the cessation of mining operations. For instance, lead-mining operations ceased in the Rheidol River valley in 1922, and by 1923, the river had quickly begun to recover. The faunal list numbered 29 species, up from 14 species, and the algal and bryophyte flora were considerably improved.

She also worked on relatively unpolluted waters, the Teifi to the south and the Dyfi to the north, comparing the mine-polluted rivers around Aberystwyth with those less affected by pollution.

She further worked to prove that relatively clean rivers could quickly become contaminated by mine wastes. In studies in the headwaters of the River Teifi, she discovered that within a year of a mine recommencing activities in 1924, the larvae of two mollusk species had disappeared.

She is remembered most for her textbook *Life in Inland Waters* (1928), the first freshwater ecology textbook in English. It was commissioned by British evolutionary biologist Julian Huxley, because freshwater biology was far less studied than marine biology.

The book is illustrated with photographs, tables, and graphs from Carpenter's research of Welsh rivers, and supplemented by the available European and American scientific literature. The book also contains more than 90 unattributed line drawings of invertebrates, which were likely drawn by Carpenter.

In the introduction to her book, Carpenter's passion for freshwater ecosystems shines through in her poetic description of freshwater life. She writes, "It is a world of infinite beauty, infinite variety, infinite charm; a world, too, which lies freely open for our exploration, and yet how many, even of professed biologists, have penetrated beyond its threshold."

This achievement provided the foundation for an international career in North America, starting at Illinois State, where she carried out further toxicity studies on fish, and continuing at Radcliffe College in Massachusetts. In 1930, she moved to McGill University in Canada to lecture on animal ecology. Carpenter subsequently became head of the Department of Biology

(1931-36) at Washington College on Chesapeake Bay. Ill health caused her retirement from teaching and led to her return to Britain in advance of the Second World War. However, she wasn't done—while at Liverpool University she produced a detailed study of the diet of young salmon in the River Dee.

She used chemistry and biology to assess water quality, and called for the use of science to direct conservation. Her research showed that if rivers are protected and monitored, they can recover from pollution. She also justified the importance of fresh waters in a socioeconomic context by describing the financial value of salmon sold at Billingsgate market in London as well as the human health risks of polluted water.

Carpenter also understood nature to be important in its own right. Engagement with nature, she wrote, was important for "health and a quiet mind."

There's still lots of restoration work to do in Wales where 1,300 abandoned metal mines are estimated to impact more than 125 miles of river. For example, the River Rheidol flows past the abandoned workings of the Cwm Rheidol lead mine. In the late 1960s, when the mine was closed, a major blowout of water colored the whole river an ochre orange and greatly added to the already high concentrations of lead and zinc in the river. The Rivers Clarach and Ystwyth also still carry elevated levels of lead, zinc and silver.

Kathleen Carpenter called for the protection of Welsh rivers from pollution, and her groundbreaking work is still highly relevant in the field of natural resource management in Wales. But above all, she championed the use of science in environmental management. "In every question of alleged pollution," she wrote, "the word of a biologist experienced in the study of fresh water is the only final evidence."

1910 DEBATING SOCIETY PHOTO

"In every question of alleged pollution," she wrote, "the word of a biologist experienced in the study of fresh water is the only final evidence."

1909 MAGAZINE COMMITTEE

WILMA MANKILLER

Wilma Mankiller ~ Oklahoma, USA

Photos courtesy of the
Oklahoma Historical Society

Wilma Mankiller is best known as the first woman elected Chief of the Cherokee Nation, as well as the first woman to ever be elected chief of a major American Indian tribe (note: there were other women chiefs of "minor" tribes). It was a position she held for 10 years, guiding a sovereign nation whose population more than doubled, from 68,000 to 170,000, during her tenure. Her election occurred in 1985, but she was hired in 1977 to work on an environmental science program for young Cherokees. With a background in grant writing, she soon founded the Community Development Department for the Cherokee Nation in 1981, focusing on improving access to water and housing. Her first project was to help families in the tiny community of Bell, Oklahoma, population around 400, gain access to clean water. Most residents were saddled with high unemployment and grinding poverty, and few had inside toilets or running water. The school, the only public source of clean water, was in danger of closing, and people were moving away. Those remaining had a deep distrust of any governmental agency, tribal or not, after decades of failed and misguided policies.

"One of the things my parents taught me, and I'll always be grateful...is to not ever let anybody else define me; [but] for me to define myself...I want to be remembered as the person who helped us restore faith in ourselves."

Bell needed a 16-mile-long pipeline to connect it to a clean water source, but Mankiller only had enough grant money to pay for the construction materials. Even if she had the money to hire contractors, she believed the best approach was one of self-help, allowing citizens to identify their problems and then gain control of the challenges they faced. So, she began a year-long discussion with community members on how they wanted to get water. The people in the community ultimately agreed to volunteer to build the whole pipeline, a major undertaking.

Mankiller said outsiders figured the townspeople would never volunteer to do the work, but they did. "I banked everything I ever believed in that project. Even when people were saying, 'Those people aren't ever going to show up. Half of them are on welfare. They're not going to volunteer to build their own water line in the middle of the summer, in the middle of the winter.' And I just knew they would...

"I felt that not just Cherokee people, but poor people in general, have a much greater capacity for leadership and for solving their own problems than they're given credit for. I just felt that given a chance, the people in Bell could control their own future."

She worked tirelessly with them, and she had faith in them. So, the residents set out to build the pipeline, working every day, and they completed it in eight months!

"Before that, I think people [in Bell] felt that life just happened to them. And after the project, they began to say this is my family and this is my community, and I'm responsible for it."

The project sparked similar projects across the Cherokee nation, and since 1982, there have been over a hundred projects to build waterlines, homes, and community centers.

Later, when Mankiller was elected

to serve as Chief of the Cherokee Nation in 1985, she became both the principal guardian of centuries of Cherokee tradition and customs, and chief executive of a tribe with a budget that reached $150 million a year.

She advocated relentlessly for better housing, better healthcare, and improved education. A consensus builder, she worked with the federal government to pilot a self-government agreement for the Cherokee Nation with the Environmental Protection Agency.

Throughout all this, severe injuries and health problems arose. In 1979, her vehicle was struck by an oncoming car, and she suffered broken ribs, as well as breaks in her left leg and ankle, while both her face and right leg were crushed. Initially doctors thought that she would not regain the ability to walk. After 17 operations and plastic surgery to reconstruct her face, she was released from the hospital on crutches.

Then three months after the collision, Mankiller began to notice a loss of muscle coordination. She dropped things, lost control of her eyes, had trouble chewing, couldn't grip items, and her voice tired quickly. She was soon diagnosed with myasthenia gravis, an autoimmune disease. One year after her car accident in 1980, she returned to the hospital, underwent more surgeries and began a course of chemotherapy, which lasted several years.

She rose above it all. Her many later successes earned her national recognition as the *Ms.* Magazine Woman of the Year in 1987. She was inducted into the National Women's Hall of Fame in 1993, and her autobiography, *Mankiller: A Chief and Her People*, was published the same year. In 1998, she received the Presidential Medal of Freedom, the nation's highest civilian honor.

Unfortunately, her health issues eventually caught up with her. After two kidney transplants and three bouts of cancer, she died on April 6, 2010, at age 64 from pancreatic cancer.

She's never been forgotten, however. In 2021, Cherokee Nation leaders gathered with community members in Bell to celebrate the official signing of the Wilma P. Mankiller and Charlie Soap Water Act, new legislation that is injecting at least $2 million in additional funding each year into the Cherokee Nation's efforts at eliminating continuing barriers to clean water access in the reservation.

Mankiller's father's ancestors had been forced to relocate to Indian Territory from Tennessee over the Trail of Tears in the late 1830s. Reflecting on the century and more in between, she said, "Remember that I am just a woman who is living a very abundant life. Every step I take forward is on a path paved by strong Indian women before me."

The Wilma Mankiller Quarter, minted in 2022

Photo courtesy of the Oklahoma Historical Society

Photo by C. R. Cowen, Courtesy of the Oklahoma Historical Society

"When I think of the Cherokee Nation I don't think of the government necessarily, or the structures, or the institutions, but I think of the people. And my thought is that if Cherokee People have survived such unspeakable tragedy over and over and over again throughout history, and they've managed to pick themselves up and keep moving forward and keep their vision fixed on the future, then I think future generations will do that. A simpler way of saying that is—that if you want to see our future, look at our past. We've survived all that and we're still standing...We'll be different 25 or 50 years from now. We're different than we were 25 or 50 years ago, but we'll still be here."

BRIGID
GODDESS AND SAINT

Saint Brigid ~ Ireland

The relationship between water and spirituality is likely as old as humanity itself. Throughout the world, people have consecrated wells and springs as sacred sites. The waters were frequently thought to possess miraculous healing qualities, and were often dedicated to a saint or holy person. They're among the first places where people sought the supernatural. Mircea Eliade wrote, "Water symbolizes the whole of potentiality—the source of all possible existence."

Holy wells were, and still are, a global phenomenon, but Ireland is unusual in how hundreds of these sites remain part of daily life and devotional practice. In 2014, the Irish National Monuments Service documented the location of 2,996 holy wells in the Republic of Ireland despite the loss of many of these sites in nearly every county due to farm expansion, forestry, road building, and housing and commercial developments.

Brigid served as a water goddess and held dominion over both rivers and wells. She is known as the Goddess of the Well, historically a sacred metaphor for the womb of Mother Earth from which flows life-giving water.

In Ireland, holy wells are most often springs (but sometimes ponds or entire lakes) distinct from human-excavated wells used for the collection of water. These sacred sites are commonly dedicated to a saint and their waters are "blessed with a cure" for everything from eye complaints and sore throats to head, back, tooth or stomach aches, to helping with a difficult pregnancy.

Holy wells arose from an amalgamation of pre-Christian and Christian practices, and at least one hundred holy wells were dedicated to Saint Brigid. Many of Brigid's Holy Wells still exist, some sacred to her for thousands of years, and all are said to heal disease.

There is debate about the historicity of Brigid.

Born around 451 CE, several accounts name Brigid's mother as Broicsech, a Christian from Portugal who had been captured and sold into slavery in Ireland. Brigid worked herding cattle and sheep until she joined religious life, probably in her teens, and soon became known for her remarkable generosity. Over her lifetime, she founded many churches and monasteries, and was instrumental in spreading Christianity in Ireland. Because of her work, St. Brigid was named co-patroness of Ireland along with St. Patrick.

Though a historical figure, Brigid shares her name with the pre-Christian goddess of the same name. Over the centuries, their stories have become intertwined in an intricate Celtic knot of myth and miracle. The Celtic Goddess Brigid and the Catholic Saint Brigid of Kildare both personify similar associations. Brigid was the Irish goddess of spring, fertility, life, serenity, and water, but also passion and fire. When she was not protecting mothers and newborn children, Brigid inspired many of the writers and poets for which Ireland is internationally renowned. Brigid often appeared as a fiery-haired goddess wearing a cloak of sunbeam.

The transition from goddess to saint allowed Brigid to survive within the new Christianized world where pagan beliefs —or any religious or spiritual belief system outside of Christianity—was no longer acceptable.

However, pagan roots linger at many Irish wells that were originally connected with the Celtic goddess Brigid. Brigid served as a water goddess and held dominion over both rivers and wells. She is known as the Goddess of the Well, historically a sacred metaphor for the womb of Mother Earth from which flows life-giving water. Brigid's Well in Kildare is one of the most famous sacred wells in Ireland. The well's water is said to heal any illness or wound. Though the site now belongs to St. Brigid, many still visit to seek the goddess' blessing. The Flame of Ireland burns in nearby Kildare in Brigid's honor.

Many significant wells exist near a large tree. There's a deep reverence and mythology surrounding ancient trees and wells. Following long-standing traditions, worshippers mostly visit between dusk and dawn, the time of day when the Celts believed the veil between the worlds of the living and of spirits is thinnest.

St. Brigid's feast day is celebrated every February 1st, on Imbolc, the midpoint between winter and spring. The Irish annual pilgrimage to many of Brigid's wells falls on August 1—also a cross-quarter day—or in some cases, the first Sunday in August. This is a pre-Christian Celtic holiday called Lughnasadh, after the god Lugh.

Brigid started as the Great Goddess, exalted and inseparable from the everyday activities of the Celts. Although her human avatar Saint Brigid to some degree replaced her, the church was never able to completely supplant the Goddess. Each Brigid reflects the essential spiritual values of her era, whether pagan or Christian. The "Mary of the Gael" still endures so strongly that it is now impossible to tell where the goddess ends and the saint begins.

St. Brigid's Well Kildare, County Westmeath

MARJORY STONEMAN DOUGLAS

Marjory Stoneman Douglas ~ Florida, USA

Marjory Stoneman Douglas will always be remembered as "the woman who saved the Everglades," though it was anything but easy. Born in 1890, she began working at the *Miami Herald* newspaper in 1915 as a reporter—a job she admitted she received out of pure nepotism (her father owned the paper). Because she was the only woman working there, and because it was 1915, Douglas covered the society pages.

Florida was already developing at an alarming rate. Miami was a frontier town with 5,000 people, and Governor Napoleon Bonaparte Broward's plan at the time was to drain the Everglades for development and agriculture.

After a stint as a Red Cross nurse in Europe during WWI, Douglas returned to Florida in 1920 and soon began to weave environmental concerns into her reports of garden parties and luncheons. She was later given her own column, "The Galley," which became a wildly popular pulpit for her views on women's rights, civil rights, urban planning and most anything else that interested her.

"Be depressed, discouraged, and disappointed at failure and the disheartening effects of ignorance, greed, corruption and bad politics—but never give up."

She wrote about the need for running water and sewage treatment in the burgeoning frontier city, for equal treatment and services in the African American sections of Miami, for infant and child nutrition, for women's suffrage, for city parks that preserved native plants as well as open space.

She quit the newspaper in 1923, and for the next 60+ years, Douglas supported herself as a prolific freelance writer, churning out over 100 pieces, mostly fiction. Forty of her stories ran in the *Saturday Evening Post*, many with environmental themes, settings and

characters drawn from the Everglades.

Photo courtesy of Florida Memory Project

By the early 1940s, Douglas's attention was focused on the Everglades. After five years of research on what little science existed about the vast tract of wilderness, she understood its profound importance in the ecology of South Florida, and published *The Everglades: River of Grass* in 1947. The book sold out its first printing in a month, galvanizing public interest in protecting the Everglades against development. It raised America's consciousness from perceiving wetlands as useless swamps to be drained, to environmental treasures to be preserved.

She wrote fluidly, crystallizing the beauty, diversity and fragility of the place: "There are no other Everglades in the world. They are, they have always been, one of the unique regions of the earth; remote, never wholly known. Nothing anywhere else is like them..."

Although the Everglades National Park was established the same year as

Photo courtesy of Everglades National Park

her book in 1947, throughout the 1950s, '60s and for much of the '70s, the Everglades still suffered enormous damage from drainage projects and large agricultural enterprises. Douglas railed at officials for destroying wetlands, eliminating water flows, and upsetting the natural systemic water cycles. Before most scientists were on board, she recognized that the Everglades depended not only on the flow of water from Lake Okeechobee into the park, but also upon the Kissimmee River which feeds the lake.

So, at the age of 79 in 1969, Douglas founded the Friends of the Everglades, a grassroots membership organization to help stop the construction of a proposed jetport to be built in the pristine Big Cypress region (the jetport was stopped after one runway was built, which still exists today in the Big Cypress).

During this time, she went head-to-head with government authorities. Describing her appearance in 1973 at a public meeting in Everglades City, John Rothchild wrote: "Mrs. Douglas was half the size of her fellow speakers and she wore huge dark glasses, which along with the huge

Photo courtesy of Florida Memory Project

floppy hat made her look like Scarlet O'Hara as played by Igor Stravinsky. When she spoke, everybody stopped slapping [mosquitoes] and more or less came to order. She reminded us all of our responsibility to nature and I don't remember what else. Her voice had the sobering effect of a one-room schoolmarm's. The tone itself seemed to tame the rowdiest of the local stone crabbers, plus the developers, and the lawyers on both sides. I wonder if it didn't also intimidate the mosquitoes...

The request for a Corps of Engineers permit [for the jetport] was eventually turned down. This was no surprise to those of us who'd heard her speak."

Former Assistant Secretary of the Interior Nathaniel Reed called her, "that tiny, slim, perfectly dressed, utterly ferocious grande dame who can make a redneck shake in his boots."

She said of herself, "They call me a nice old woman, but I'm not...I'm an old lady. I've got white hair, I've been around here forever, and no one can afford to be rude to me. And don't think I don't take advantage of that. I say outrageous things and get away with it.

"Be a nuisance where it counts," she said. "But don't be a bore at any time... Do your part to inform and stimulate the public to join your action...Be depressed, discouraged, and disappointed at failure and the disheartening effects of ignorance, greed, corruption and bad politics—but never give up.

"I would be very sad if I had not fought. I'd have a guilty conscience if I had been here and watched all this happen to the environment and not been on the right side," she said. In 1991, at the age of 101

Photo courtesy of Florida Memory Project

and still fighting, she was asked how she persisted to reach goals that seemed distant or even unattainable. Her answer was, "Why should I give up?"

The National Park now boasts the largest protected stand of sawgrass in North America, the largest protected mangrove ecosystem in the western hemisphere, and important habitat for 21 federally threatened and endangered species. Recognizing such values, Congress designated nearly 1.3 million acres of the park as wilderness in 1978, affording it the highest level of protection possible. In a nod to her tireless work, the entire area was eventually christened the Marjory Stoneman Douglas Wilderness. In her lifetime, the Everglades went from a wilderness on the brink of irreparable development, to a National Park, a Wetland of International Significance, an International Biosphere Preserve, and a legislatively designated wilderness area.

In 1996, Florida voters additionally passed a constitutional amendment that held polluters primarily responsible for cleaning up the Everglades.

Douglas was awarded the Presidential Medal of Freedom in 1993, at the age of 103, by President Clinton. After her death in 1998, her ashes were scattered over the wilderness area and her house and property have since been maintained by the Florida Park Service as a lasting memorial to a remarkable "woman who saved the Everglades." Marjory Stoneman Douglas was posthumously inducted into the National Women's Hall of Fame on October 7, 2000.

Photo courtesy of Florida Memory Project

"I would be very sad if I had not fought. I'd have a guilty conscience if I had been here and watched all this happen to the environment and not been on the right side."

Photo courtesy of Everglades National Park

WATER AND WOMEN ORGANIZATIONS

350.org: *https://350.org*
African Center for Aquatic Sciences: *https://www.agl-acare.org*
African Women in Science: *https://www.agl-acare.org/program-awis*
Champions of the Earth: *https://www.unep.org/championsofearth/*
Council of Popular and Indigenous Organizations of Honduras (COPINH):
http://copinhenglish.blogspot.com/p/who-we-are.html
Dreamcatcher Charity: *https://www.dreamcatchercharity.org*
For the Earth and Water: *https://www.facebook.com/LivingWaterWalk*
Friends of Lake Turkana: *https://www.friendsoflaketurkana.org/index.php/en/*
Global Water Partnership: *https://www.gwp.org*
Global Water Policy Project: *www.globalwaterpolicy.org*
Gorongosa National Park: *https://gorongosa.org*
Keepers of the Water: *https://www.keepersofthewaters.org*
Lake Baikal Foundation: *https://baikalfoundation.ru/en/*
Mission Blue: *https://missionblue.org*
National Women's History Museum:
https://www.womenshistory.org/education-resources/biographies/marjory-stoneman-douglas
Nibi Walk: *http://www.nibiwalk.org/about/*
Oceanswell: *https://oceanswell.org*
Our Gorongosa (coffee): *https://ourgorongosa.com*
Polar Impact Network: *https://www.polarimpactnetwork.org*
Stockholm International Water Institute (SIWI): *https://siwi.org*
The Arctic Institute: *https://www.thearcticinstitute.org*
The Goldman Environmental Prize: *https://www.goldmanprize.org*
The Nature Conservancy: *https://www.nature.org/en-us/*
The Tonga Voyaging Society: *https://www.nativeland.org/mnf-tonga-voyaging-society*
The Water Project: *https://thewaterproject.org*
Utthan: *https://utthangujarat.org*
UW-Madison Center for Limnology: *https://limnology.wisc.edu*
Water for Women: *https://www.waterforwomenfund.org/en/index.aspx*
Water.org: *https://water.org*
We the People of Detroit: *https://www.wethepeopleofdetroit.com*
Women's Earth Alliance: *https://womensearthalliance.org*

ADDITIONAL WATER ORGANIZATIONS AND RESOURCES

350.org: *https://350.org*

500 Women Scientists: *https://500womenscientists.org*

A Mighty Girl: Guardians of the Planet: *https://www.amightygirl.com/blog?p=11863&fbclid=IwAR1kLKp3j_FnX-*

Arctic Relations, Scholarship & Stories: *https://www.arctic-relations.info*

Asian Development Blog: *https://blogs.adb.org*

Black in Marine Science: *https://www.blackinmarinescience.org*

Black Mesa Trust: *https://www.blackmesatrust.org*

Eco-Governance: *https://www.codes.earth*

Gender is Not Plan B: *https://www.genderisnotplanb.com*

Global Lake Ecological Observatory Network: *http://blog.gleon.org*

Global Water Partnership: *https://www.gwp.org/en/*

Inspiring Girls Expeditions: *https://www.inspiringgirls.org*

International Arctic Research Center: *https://uaf-iarc.org*

International Institute for Sustainable Development: *https://www.iisd.org*

International Water Association: *https://iwa-network.org*

Keepers of the Water: *https://www.keepersofthewaters.org*

Run for Salmon: *http://run4salmon.org*

Science Moms: *https://sciencemoms.com*

Scientific Committee on Antarctic Research: *https://www.scar.org*

Sea Women of Melanesia: *www.seawomen.net*

Seventh Generation Fund for Indigenous Peoples: *https://7genfund.org*

Sister Water Project: *https://www.osfdbq.org/sister-water-project-main/sister-water-project/*

Sitka Sound Science Center: *https://sitkascience.org*

Society for Women in Marine Science: *https://swmsmarinescience.com*

Spirit Aligned Leadership: *https://spiritaligned.org*

Sustainable Ocean Alliance: *https://www.soalliance.org*

The Arctic Institute: *https://www.thearcticinstitute.org*

The Shackleton Medal: *https://shackleton.com/en-us/pages/shackleton-medal*

Urban Ocean Lab: *https://urbanoceanlab.org*

UW-Milwaukee School of Freshwater Sciences: *https://uwm.edu/freshwater/*

Water for Women: *https://www.waterforwomenfund.org/en/index.aspx*

Water Museums Global Network: *https://www.watermuseums.net*

Waterkeepers Alliance: *https://waterkeeper.org*

Wetlands International: *https://www.wetlands.org*

Women in Ocean Science: *https://www.womeninoceanscience.com*

Women in the Arctic and Antarctic: *https://womeninthearcticandantarctic.ca*

Women of the Water: *https://www.womenofthewater.org*

Women4Oceans: *https://www.women4oceans.org*

World Water Day: *https://www.worldwaterday.org*

Youth4Ocean Forum: *https://maritime-forum.ec.europa.eu/en/frontpage/1484*

Youth for Water and Climate: *https://youthwaterclimate.org*

CONTACT INFORMATION

To contact Mary Burns:
burnsbates@gmail.com

Website:
www.manitowishriverstudio.com

Please contact Mary:
If you know of a venue to host this exhibit.

If you know of other women who could be included in this exhibit.

How you can help:
Donate to the resources listed.

Get involved in the water organizations listed or in your local community.

Thank you!!

Watercolors

Hand-dyed Indigo Panels Celebrating Shades of Water

In this exhibit hand-dyed indigo panels celebrate some of the many shades of water from light aquamarine to dark stormy seas.

These panels of silk and cotton were hand-dyed in indigo with several different dyeing techniques. The lightest shades were created with fresh leaves from our own home-grown indigo plants (*Persicaria tinctoria*). A darker grouping of cotton panels were vat dyed with my sister Nancy Burns and my daughter Callie Bates, of Hazel Eyes Textiles.

And an additional larger panel was dyed in an indigo fermentation vat by master dyer Debbie Ketchum Jircik, Circle of Life Studio in Eagle River, Wisconsin.

My deep thanks go to those who over centuries created the indigo dyeing traditions.

ACKNOWLEDGEMENTS

I am thankful to water in all forms, without which none of life would exist.

I am very grateful to all the women represented in the exhibit, and all of the people and organizations worldwide protecting our waters.

Thanks to my family, friends and supporters of this adventure.

Special thanks to the Wisconsin Arts Board and the National Endowment for the Arts; Trout Lake Station, Center for Limnology-University of Wisconsin and Gretchen Gerrish, Susan Knight, Terry Daulton; Steve Greenberg and Pointcarré Textile Software; Vibeke Vestby of Digital Weaving Norway; the amazingly creative and patient Bev Watkins of Watkins Graphic Design for the beautiful layout and design of this book; Jim Schumaker, photography; Mitch Myers, framing; Simon Stevenoski of Oski Fabrication for creating our awesome new display; Kip Evans for the use of his photo of Sylvia Earle which I used as a basis for her weaving; Anne Laure Camilleri for the use of her photo of Tinker Schuman which I used as a basis for her weaving; Stephanie Peltier; Tasha Beeds and the family of Josephine Mandamin-Ba; Christy Butterfield for connecting me to Aunofo Havea; The Goldman Environmental Prize, Ellen Lomonico; Stephanie Smith and Angela Nankabirwa; Peter McKeever; the amazing and generous staff at Gorongosa National Park; Tina Kuckkahn; Debbie Ketchum Jircik; Louise Karpinski; Virginia Thomas; Mike O'Connell; Catherine Duigan; Kristina Kiehl and Sydney Morris; the Oklahoma Historical Society; to my sisters; and to all others who have helped support and/or fund this project.

Thank you to the very talented Callie Bates for editing all of our written components in the exhibit. And deep gratitude to my husband John Bates for writing the text, for his unwavering support and believing in the vision of this exhibit and of me. You are my rock and light in the world.

~~~

ABOUT THE WEAVER, MARY E. BURNS

Mary Burns expresses her love of northern woodlands and waters in her weavings and writings. An award-winning weaver, Mary creates weavings, feltings and eco-printed work that reflect the hues and patterns of the natural world. Her jacquard loom, a TC-2 that she's named Brigid Mariah, allows her to craft her work in exceptional detail, vibrancy, and character.

Mary gathers inspiration from many places and cultures. Her looms include two Jacquard looms and a Cranbrook rug loom. She teaches an array of textile art classes as well.

Her *Ancestral Women Exhibit: Wisconsin's Twelve Tribes*, which honors and celebrates one woman from each of Wisconsin's 12 Native American Tribes, was completed in 2016, and continues to tour. Please see *https://ancestralwomen.com* for more information.

Her work has been displayed in numerous exhibits and shows, including several art and science collaborations. She has also participated in several art and science residencies.

Mary is also a writer. Her first novel Heartwood (2003) is a fantasy/natural history novel for young adults. She is a contributor to *A Place to Which We Belong: Wisconsin Writers on Wisconsin Landscapes* (1998).

Mary's love of weaving started in high school art class and has only continued to grow over time. Mary and her family have lived in her grandparents' home on the Manitowish River in northern Wisconsin since 1984.

She's honored to do the work she now does.

Please note: None of the pieces in Mary's *Ancestral Women Exhibit* or her *Women and Water Exhibit* are for sale. Cultural appropriation is a very real concern, and every effort has been made to honor these women in a good and right way.

~~~

CPSIA information can be obtained
at www.ICGtesting.com
Printed in the USA
JSHW071538070623
42805JS00003B/8